CREATING FICTION

National Writing Institute

ISBN 1-888-344-01-6

Manufactured in the United States of America

For information, write: National Writing Institute
                            624 W. University #248
                            Denton, TX 76201-1889

                            call: 1 (800) 688-5375
                            e-mail: info@writingstrands.com

NATIONAL WRITING INSTITUTE PUBLICATIONS

STUDENTS

Writing Strands Level 1
Writing Strands Level 2
Writing Strands Level 3
Writing Strands Level 4
Writing Strands Level 5
Writing Strands Level 6
Writing Strands Level 7
Writing Exposition
Creating Fiction

Communication And Interpersonal Relationships

Dragonslaying Is For Dreamers
Axel Meets The Blue Men
Axel's Challenge

PARENTS/TEACHERS

Evaluating Writing

Reading Strands

Analyzing The Novel:
Dragonslaying Is For Dreamers

Essays on Writing

Dear Fellow Writer,

Everything you need to know about creative writing cannot be put in one book or really ever written anywhere. There's way too much involved. But, any book on writing can give you some of the tools that you'll need.

All good writers have learned from other writers. Writers read. This is one of the basic truths about this very hard thing that you've decided to do. When people read, they absorb the rhythms of the language. When they read well written material, they begin to feel how the language is used well. There really is no other way to acquire that feeling for words and how they flow together. What you'll need to do is to get reading lists from your library. They all have them. Lists recommended for college bound students would be a good place to start.

In this short book there are exercises that I've used for years with my students in high school and college. Their use here doesn't mean that they're perfect or that you should write like these students have. They're examples of what these students did with the directions in the exercises.

If you feel you do better at the exercises than the examples, wonderful. If you don't write as well as some of the examples, don't worry about it. You and the students who wrote the examples have had different experiences and all beginning writers have skills that are based on their experiences.

If you want to write stories, that's fine. Do so. The exercises in this book will give you skills in the areas of fiction writing that you'll need. There is no listing of objectives or suggested time frames to these exercises. Take as long as you need to. Learning to write is not easy nor can it be accomplished quickly. The important things are reading well written books, practicing your skills at writing and maintaining your desire to write.

Writers aren't like other people, they're artists. Artists see situations differently than the rest of us do. That's their job, to reflect what they see in the culture to others. I like to think that artists have a special place in any culture. I feel they have a responsibility to others to use their perceptive and creative intelligence in their observations of what is called the human condition and then to show to others what they've learned.

This isn't a bad way for you to start to think about writing. You've an interest in people, and you're creative or you wouldn't want to write. Writers observe and note actions, situations, characters, relationships, and scenes. These they used in their fiction to tell their readers what they understand. What this means is that you must have something to say before you can write well. Good fiction is much more than just the relating of a series of events. There's understanding of all of these conditions involved in the series of events.

In your observations, you'll have learned something about what it means to be human and alive (the human condition). Good writers don't tell their readers what they understand. Rather, they write stories that contain this understanding, and perceptive readers "pick up" this understanding. This may not make much sense now, but it will when you've finished this book.

Writing is very hard and often painful, but it's never boring. It's frustrating, and at times you'll want to scream at your pen or word processor. Do it. It helps. There'll be times you'll want to cry and times you will. There will be other times you'll find yourself laughing right out loud. Wonderful. What a great way to spend time. Have fun with these exercises. Read, write and work with language and your life will never be without challenge or lack excitement.

Dave Marks

CONTENTS   page

1

Establishing Location for Your Narrative Voice

If you've been studying writing, you'll be familiar with the idea that, as an author, you must speak to your reader, but you know you can't do so directly and so must create a voice to speak for you. This speaker is called the narrative voice. What is read on the page are your words but your words spoken by the voice you have created to represent what you want your reader to know.

Usually there will be limits to what your narrative voice can tell your reader. There can be very strict limitations on what your voice reveals, but sometimes you will want almost no restrictions on your voice. You might choose to have your voice be a character in your story. If this is the case, the voice belongs to a character through whom the story is being told. If this is so, this voice has limits in the point of view choices. You might want to check back to the section on point of view.

This voice, that of a character, cannot see everything or know everything. For instance, your story cannot move from place to place any more easily than your character/voice could move or see things that a real character could see. Your voice will be restricted in the same way that a real person would be.

In this exercise you will experience giving limits to your narrative voices' accounts of an accident on the corner of First and Eagle Street. You will create five voices, four of these will be characters in the action. The fifth voice will speak as a non-character in a non-involved, objective, third person and omnipresent voice. Because the first four voices will be characters, they'll be limited in knowledge of the accident to what they could see or hear during the action. The last voice, of course, will have no such limitation.

The first four accounts of the accident will be in first person, because they'll be accounts told by characters who were witnesses to the accident or were in it.

The first narrative voice will be a boy on a bicycle. He's heading north on First Street. What he sees during the accident will be limited by where he is.

The second narrative voice will be a little old lady who is walking her dog and waiting to cross First Street. They're standing on the south-east corner of Eagle and First. What she can tell of the accident must be limited to what could be seen from that position.

The third narrative voice will be a boy who is riding in the back seat of an old car traveling east on Eagle. What he can tell must be limited by what he can see from the back seat.

The fourth narrative voice will be a fireman who is riding in a fire truck traveling south on First and about to turn right (west) on Eagle. What he can tell of the accident must be limited to what he can see and hear form the right seat of the truck.

The fifth narrative voice will be a non-character who will assume an omnipresent position. This means that this voice will be able to be in many places at once. What this voice will be able to tell about the accident will not be limited by line of sight. But, it'll not be omniscient, so it'll not know what the participants in the accident are thinking.

The four involved narrative voices should speak in first person, employ past tense, be subjective and be limited in knowledge and perspective. The fifth voice, the non-involved narrative voice, should speak in third person, employ past tense, be objective and be limited in knowledge but not in perspective. Again, if these terms are not clear to you, check the "Point of View"exercise.

As in any narrative, you must understand the limitations of the characters. It's not a bad idea for you to map out the rooms and locations of the actions in all of your writing. It's easy to make mistakes in sight lines or positions unless you use such a guide. It'll help you to understand the limitations of the sight lines of the first four narrative voices if you draw a map of the corner of First and Eagle. Draw the buildings, trees and bushes.

You should mark the positions of the bike, fire truck, car and the old lady with the dog before the accident. You should then position the characters just after the accident. This will make it clear in your mind just what sight-line limits each of the characters have. You will find helpful the diagram provided later in this exercise.

Your job in this narration is to tell of the accident, but to do it in such a way that the logical sight perspectives of the narrative voices are not violated. The reader should not be told something by an involved narrative voice which that narrator, as a character, could not know.

An example of this limitation is seen by examining what the old lady could and could not see before, during and after the accident. If, during the accident, the boy on the bicycle falls under the fire truck and slides to its far side, away from the lady, she would be able to see the boy when he stops sliding. She might be able to see the car. She would be able to see the driver of the truck when he get gets out, but she would not be able to see the other firemen in the truck when he gets out on the far side of the truck. If this narrative voice limitation is clear to the reader, the writing will make much more sense than it would if the reader were confused by not understanding where the lady is before and during the accident.

Of course, there is no page limit to what you should write. A good rule is never to write more than you have to or more than your reader would like to or need to know. You do have to be sure the sight-line limits are clear to your reader. You should try to capture the character, age and personality of each of the first four narrative voices. You can do this by having them describe the accident as people their ages would talk. You surely don't want all four descriptions to sound like you talking.

You are to write of an accident that happens between the fire truck and the old Buick. This is not to be a big crash. The boy on the bike is to be involved in some way.

Here again are the positions of the five voices at the time of the accident:

1. Boy on Bike - Going north of First Street heading toward the intersection of First and Eagle.
2. Old Lady - Standing on the south-west corner of First and Eagle.
3. Fireman - In fire truck going south on First and entering the intersection of First and Eagle. At the time of the accident the truck is turning right onto West Eagle.
4. Boy in Car - Riding in the back seat of the car going east on Eagle. The car is about to enter the intersection.
5. Non-involved Voice - Has a bird's-eye view of the corner of First and Eagle. This means that the voice has a view from above the accident and can see everything that happens.

BEFORE   **AFTER**

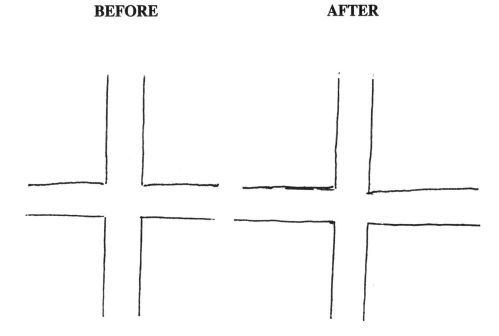

3

2

Further Exercises
in
Establishing Narrative Voice Position

It's important that an author be able to locate the position from which the narrative voice speaks to the reader. This position will determine what the voice can tell the reader about the scene and action. In learning to do this you will also have an opportunity to learn some other skills, if you'd like to. You should have some practice in creating mood and in structuring your prose so that your reader can easily create meaning.

There are two choices an author has in establishing position for narrative voice:
1. One position (called narrative voice position) has to do with the point of view and the restrictions authors impose upon themselves.
2. The other position (narrator location) is that place from which the narrative voice can observe the action it chooses to describe.

The author, in establishing narrative voice position, has a number of choices. If the narrative voice's point of view is limited, the narrator location has to be restricted to the limits set by the situation. If the narrative voice's point of view is omnipresent, then there are no restrictions on the location, and it may even be changed from time to time. These narrator locations determine how the scene is described.

This exercise deals with the narrator location and how it can be handled. If the piece is to be a description of, say, a ferris wheel, the narrator can be in any number of places when it describes the scene. The thing you must realize is that, no matter what type of voice you use, the narrator must be seeing and describing the ferris wheel from some actual, physical place. The place may change, and that is one of the things you will learn to do in this exercise, but you must keep in mind that any changes in the narrator location must be accompanied by changes in the sight lines used by the narrative voice in description.

If the narrative position in your description of the ferris wheel is omnipresent, the narrator location can shift from the line waiting to board the ride to the booth where the tickets are sold and then to the wheel itself as it rotates. In this case, there'd be three completely different descriptions of the riders and the ride, because each of the locations would have different sight lines, and the narrator would have a different view of the ferris wheel from the three positions. The omnipresent point of view allows the author to move from the ticket booth to the top of the wheel but does not allow the author to describe the scene from the top of the wheel if the narrator location is in the booth.

Write three descriptive paragraphs of a ferris wheel. All three will be third person, plural, past tense, objective, non-involved and limited in knowledge. All three will be related in that they'll describe the same continuing event. Have the narrator location start in the ticket booth, shift to the line waiting to board the ride and then shift to the ride itself.

Check again the narrative voice options I have given you for each of the voices:
- Third person (he, she, they)
- Plural (they)
- Past tense (went, did, saw)
- Objective (not caring what happens)
- Non-involved (not part of any action or scene)
- Limited in knowledge: (only knows what can be seen, and is not in the minds of characters)

As examples of how the voice's location determines the sight lines of the narrative voice, note the differences in the following passages about a customer seen entering a store from a) the sidewalk, and b) inside the store.

   a) *He stood looking into the store window, then without turning, went through the open doorway.* In this case the narrator location must have been outside of the store, maybe across the street, because of the use of *went*. This word indicates the subject, *he*, moved from an established position to one further away from the narrator's viewing place.

   b) *He stood looking into the store window, then without turning, came in the open doorway.* In this case, the use of *came* indicates the narrator must have been inside the store when the man entered.

In this exercise you should have some practice creating mood. The creation of mood is very difficult for beginning writers, so don't worry if you find it hard and get frustrated, because, with this exercise, you, at least, will gain an understanding of the complexity of the process and learn to appreciate when others do it well.

Mood is established, in part, by controlling the following factors:
1. Setting
2. Character attitude toward place, situation, other characters
3. Colors and patterns
4. The orientation and size of structures
5. Light and shadow
6. Movement
7. Dialogue

8. Sentence length and variety
9. Narrator attitude

You should be aware of how all of the above elements work in creating mood. The following exercise will give you experience in using these nine factors.

Structure for "Car Crash"

You are to write just three paragraphs:

1. A paved country road makes a sharp bend near a very large oak tree. A mother robin lives in the tree with her three chicks.

2. A young man driving a new sports car runs into the tree.

3. After the crash, the robin finds one of her chicks has been thrown out of the nest and continues to feed the remaining two.

The **narrator location shifts** from the **tree in the first** paragraph, to the **car in the second,** back to the **tree in the last few sentences of the second** and **stays there for all of the third paragraph.**

PARAGRAPH ONE:

Point of View:	Third person plural, past tense, objective attitude and non-involved observer
Narrator Location:	As if the narrator were standing near the tree.
Mood of Scene:	Peace and tranquility.
Event:	After the scene is set, the mood is established and the mother robin makes three trips to the ground in search of worms. In the distance there is the high-pitched scream of tortured rubber as a car slides on pavement.

Establishing the Mood:

1. **Setting -**	It is a warm spring evening on a paved but little-used country road. The only house visible is at least half a mile away.
2. **Colors and patterns -**	Use colors that are soft, such as light green and light blue. The bark on

6

the oak is a soft, furry brown. The setting sun casts long filigreed shadows across the meadow and the roadside.

3. **Shapes, Sizes and Lines -** The reader's attention should focus on the one big tree. There should be no sharp corners or movements. The oak is the only thing of size in the near vicinity. The smoke from the chimney of the distant house rises straight up in a thin line then dissipates in the clear air.

4. **Sentence Length and Variety -** You want your reader to recognize the patterns that nature has set here. This will be important later when man's technology interferes and then the pattern reestablishes itself. The mother robin's three trips to the ground should all be described in one sentence, but each trip should be described in detail. This will set a pattern expanded upon later in the third paragraph. This example should make this clear:

The mother robin, after a long curving glide, landed near the base of the tree and, after a few light hops, stood still, her head cocked to one side as she listened for movement below the ground, stabbed her beak into the soft grasses and dirt and pulled out most of a long earthworm, which she took back to her wildly chirping chicks, who, after having eaten, were not quiet; and this forced her to launch herself again to the ground, alighting near the roadside, where she. . .

Things you should try to avoid:
1. Putting lots of animals in the scene: deer, rabbits, chipmunks and even moose.
2. Personifying the tree: *The great oak spread her arms to protect the birds. . .*
3. Putting fleecy clouds in the sky.
4. Labeling the scene as peaceful and tranquil. *It was a beautiful day, peaceful and. . .*
5. Giving the mother robin noble motives and thoughts: *The mother robin, though tired, knew her chicks deserved another worm, and so she decided to make one last trip to the ground before the sun set.* (Mother robins do not think nor are they noble.)
6. Having the robins hatched in the late summer or fall, and having a squirrel gathering nuts or a farmer cutting corn in the spring.
7. Having the narrative voice say, *A screech of tires was heard,* for there is no one there and the narrative voice is not omniscient and can't know what the robins can hear.
8. Making subjective value judgments: *It was a nice day. . .* You cannot do this for the narrative voice must be objective.

PARAGRAPH TWO:

Point of View: Third person singular, present tense, subjective attitude, non-involved and limited omniscient knowledge.

         -Third person (he, they, it)

         -Present tense (it is, he sees, it leans)

         -Subjective attitude (voice enjoys the experience and cares about what happens)

         -Non-involved (not part of the action, not as a person in the car)

         -Limited omniscient knowledge (can tell of other's thoughts and actions)

Narrator
Location: This scene should be described as if the narrative voice is inside the car next to the driver and then shifts to the ground near the tree for the last few sentences of the paragraph. You will have to remember that the narrative voice is **not** a passenger in the car. The narrative voice does not represent a person. There is only one person in the car, and he's the driver, and he is **not** the narrative voice.

Mood of Scene
and Action: Fun-loving and exciting

Event: A young man is driving his new sports car on an empty country road. When the paragraph begins, he's a good two or three miles from the curve near the big tree. He enjoys driving the car on the curving and hilly blacktopped road. There is a long straightway, maybe half of a mile long, in the road leading to the curve by the tree. He opens the car up to see what it will do, and for some reason (you will have to invent it) loses control and hits the tree. The force of the impact jars one of the baby birds out of the nest and it falls near the wreck. After the impact there is a great silence.

Establishing the Mood:

1. Setting: The young man is alone and enjoys driving his new car on the country road in the late afternoon.

2. Color and
   patterns: At the speed he's driving, the trees along the sides of the road form a long, blurred, green tunnel. The sun, low in the west, flashes like a strobe light through the leaves. The black surface races towards him, and the white center stripes seem to be one continuous line. A description of these colors and patterns should give your reader a sense of speed and excitement in the young man's use of the superbly engineered piece of machinery.

8

3. Sentence Length
   and Variety: On the straight stretches of the road the sentences should lengthen, and on the curves, when the driver must slow down by shifting and braking, the sentences should get shorter and choppier. On the final, long straightaway, just before the curve near the big tree, the sentences should be long, and, when the driver loses control of the car, they should get progressively shorter until the point of impact. This is to give the reader a feeling for the rhythm of the ride by having the sentence length correspond to the speed of the time passing in the various portions of the trip.

4. Movement: To help the reader feel the excitement of the ride, the experiences the driver feels should be described. The surge forward when the driver shifts into a lower gear to slow for the curves and the pressure back into the leather seat when the driver accelerates should be carefully detailed. The reader should feel the wind and the centrifugal force that presses him to the side in the curves, and he should hear the howl of the engine, the whine of the gear box and the scream of the tires on the pavement.

   When the driver loses control and the car spins, the reader should see the trees and the road spin past the windshield and hear the gravel bang and clatter up under the body when the car leaves the pavement and slides on the shoulder. There should be the lurch and bounce into the air when the car leaves the roadway and crosses over the ditch and the bank by the tree.

5. Dialogue: The driver can talk to himself and to the car. Many of us do this when we're alone and excited. It is important that the reader sees that the young man is enjoying the ride, and the reader should enjoy it right along with him. If you want to, you could have the driver keep a running commentary on the car and the drive. It might read like this:

   "Okay, Baby, one more curve before the long straightaway. Let's settle down and take hold on this one. Eighty-five is a little hot, ease off. . .there, that's better. Seventy-eight and into fourth and down to sixty-five. . . still too high. Hunker down, Sweetheart, 'cause here's third. She's holding like she had fingertips—beee-utiful. There it is, fifty and accelerate out into the straightaway—sixty. . .sixty-five, back into fourth and seventy-five and fifth, and let's see what you can do, Sweetheart. You've got about a mile of clean road on your nose—let's go!" He reaches into the glove box for a package of gum and presses out one wrapped stick. He manages to remove the gum stick, but, unfortunately, he drops the package on the floor.

It's important to this piece that the reader enjoy the technology the car represents, so you should describe in detail the driving of the car and the mechanics of high speed. If you've not driven a car at high speed, **do not do so for this exercise**. Ask someone what it's like.

To have the reader enjoy the thrill of the ride, the driver cannot be drunk or high on drugs. He must have a good bit of skill at driving and drive fast but not crazily, for that would destroy the joy of the ride for the reader.

Just before the impact, the narrator position must shift from inside of the car to what it was in the first paragraph, next to the tree.

At the point of the impact, the car will stop at the tree, but there will be pieces of the car which will fly past the tree. The mirrors, hubcaps, pieces of glass, chrome trim and liquid from the radiator will continue on by both sides of the tree and land beyond it.

Directly after the impact, one of the front wheels may spin for a minute, and one of the hubcaps may roll onto the gravel at the side of the road. After the pieces all have stopped moving and there is the great silence which always follows a tremendous crash, a small bit of glass may fall from the windshield and tinkle on a twisted piece of body metal before the dripping of the liquid starts. Remember that the second paragraph is in present tense, which will give an immediacy to the action. The narrative voice in this paragraph is subjective. If the narrative voice enjoys the experience of the ride, the reader is more likely to enjoy it also.

If you have had someone you know hurt in a car crash recently, you might want to skip the next section of this assignment. If you do read it, it will give you a picture that is not nice to think about, but it might make you more careful when you drive or ride with someone who likes to drive fast.

The following figures may give you some idea of the nature of the impact of a car at high speed. Studies at Yale and Cornell Universities found what happens when a car hits a tree at just 55 miles per hour:

1. At 1/10ths of a second, the front bumper and the grillwork collapse.
2. At 2/10ths of a second, the hood crumbles, rises, smashes into the windshield and the grillwork disintegrates.
3. At 3/10ths of a second, the driver is sprung upright from his seat, his broken knees pressed against the dashboard, the steering wheel bends under his grip.
4. At 4/10ths of a second, the front of his car is destroyed and dead still, but the rear end is still plunging forward at 55 mph.—the half-ton motor crunches into the tree.
5. At 5/10ths of a second, the driver's hands bend the steering column into an almost vertical position and he's impaled on the steering wheel shaft. Steel punctures his lungs and arteries.
6. At 6/10 of a second, the impact rips the shoes off his feet. The chassis bends in the middle

and the driver's head is slammed into the windshield. The car's rear begins its downward fall as its spinning wheels churn into the ground.

7. At 7/10ths of a second, the entire body of the car is twisted out of shape. The front seat rams forward, pinning the driver against the steering shaft. Blood spurts from his mouth. Shock has frozen his heart.

PARAGRAPH THREE

1. Point of View: Third person plural, past tense, objective attitude and non-involved observer.

2. Narrator
   Location: At the side of the tree as in the first paragraph and in the last few sentences of the second.

Establishing the Mood: The gradual returning to the peace and tranquility of the first paragraph.

1. Color and patterns - The shadows lengthen as the sun sets, and the colors mellow and fade into each other. The area takes on a green and golden glow.
2. Light and shadow - The low sun puts spots of light on the trunk of the large tree and the darkening surface of the road.
3. Movement - Just after the crash there is no movement, but soon the mother robin flies to the ground to look at the fallen chick. She then resumes the pattern of her hunting for the last worms of the day.
4. Sounds - After the crash, all the normal sounds of the roadside in spring stop. The first sounds to resume would be from insects. Then the birds would begin to call.

Things you should watch for:
1. Because you will find it difficult, you will want to skip the emphasis on the silence after the crash. Don't.
2. Remember that the robin's search for worms in the last paragraph parallels the patterns in the first paragraph but does not use the same phrases and wording.
3. The narrative voice is to be objective, so you are not to mourn the plight of the driver or the baby bird in the third paragraph.

Interpretation of literature is complicated, but, as a writer, you should be aware of the elements of what you have written and how they're open to interpretation by a reader. I've carefully structured this three-paragraph exercise for you. When you write, you should be as careful with structure as I've been.

You should examine your narrative so as to be able to answer the following questions:

1. What forces are at play in the first paragraph? You should recognize among others:
   A. Birth
   B. Raising young
   C. Growth
   D. Seasonal change

2. What label can be given to this list? (Think of what connections there are in the items in the list.)

3. What force is present in a major way in the second paragraph? You may suggest physical forces like centrifugal force, inertia, or gravity, but the major literary force in the second paragraph has to do with the idea of the boy and the car as they represent man and his love of technology and the natural forces men cannot control.

4. What happens when these two forces collide in the last part of the second paragraph, and how greatly does this affect the rhythm and pattern set up in the first paragraph but resumed in the third?

The answers to the above questions should give you a good start on an understanding of what an interpretation of your piece might suggest.

3

Senses

In your descriptive passages, it's important that you control what your readers feels about what you're showing them. One of the ways to do this is to appeal to the senses; that is to use concrete words and describe what things *look, taste, sound,* and *feel* like. You must take into consideration what you want your readers to feel when you describe places or things and include those sensory experiences which will help you get your job done.

As practice, you might write two descriptive pieces using as few abstractions as possible and creating in your readers a distinctly different feeling for each one. You should, in this first exercise, concentrate on just one of the senses. Descriptions employing the sense of sight might include the following elements:
1. Color
    A. Hue
    B. Intensity
    C. Contrast
    D. Pattern
    E. Shading
2. Shape
3. Size
4. Spatial relationship
5. Directional orientation

This exercise will be much easier for you if you pick something to describe that you're familiar with and can look at as you write. Think of two people who would feel differently about a thing: such as a large lawn as seen by the proud owner, and then as seen by the boy who has to mow it. Or your kitchen before you or someone in your family starts to cook for a large dinner party, and the same room just after dinner when it has to be cleaned up.

I like to organize ideas before I begin to write. This might help you also. I don't use a formal outline, but I do make lists and groups of ideas on scrap paper. My notes for this exercise might look like this:

The two feelings I would like to create:

A. _____

B. _____

What I'll describe to produce feeling A:

_____

_____

What I'll describe to produce feeling B:

_____

_____

When you have a feeling for this exercise, after doing these partial descriptions, you should practice using all of the senses for your reader. Your reader should not be told that the peach was juicy, rather, as the readers sink their teeth into the soft skin, they should feel the cool juice from the almost-too-ripe peach gush and run down their chins onto their fingers.

You can create exercises for yourself employing the other senses. Sound can have the following major characteristics:
1. Volume
2. Tone
3. Duration
4. Pitch
5. Intensity
6. Rhythm or patterns

Touch can determine the following characteristics:
1. Heat (differences in temperature)
2. Pressure
3. Texture
4. Size
5. Contour
6. Degree of water content (wet or dry)
7. Flexibility
8. Friction (slippery or sticky)

Taste can indicate only four characteristics:
1. Sweet
2. Sour
3. Salt
4. Bitter

For taste, you will have to include the sense of touch as it is associated with eating: soft, hard, brittle, crunchy, slick, greasy, mushy, crisp, limp, flaky, and so on.

When you think you're ready, you should write a more complicated piece of description employing as many of the senses as you can manage. This description should combine the senses, that is, you should not have a paragraph of sight and then one of sound. Rather, they should be dealt with simultaneously. You should decide before you start how you want your readers to feel about what you write.

4

Cheerleader / Point of View

There are two kinds of point of view, but it's not likely for you to be confused by them. One is the attitude the author or the narrative voice takes toward the subject or the situation. This becomes apparent when the narrative voice talks directly to the reader and makes clear how the author or the narrative voice feels, or when the narrative voice is extremely serious or flippant. The other point of view, the one that is so important for beginning writers to master, has to do with the options the author has for the conditions of the narrative voice. The chart below shows these options.

<table>
<tr><td colspan="4" align="center">NARRATIVE VOICE
POINT OF VIEW CHOICES</td></tr>
<tr><td>Person:</td><td>First</td><td>Second</td><td>Third</td></tr>
<tr><td></td><td>Singular or Plural</td><td>"you"</td><td>Singular or Plural</td></tr>
<tr><td>Tense:</td><td>Past</td><td>Present</td><td>Future</td></tr>
<tr><td>Attitude:</td><td>Objective</td><td></td><td>Subjective</td></tr>
<tr><td>Involvement:</td><td>Part of Action</td><td></td><td>Observer</td></tr>
<tr><td>Knowledge:</td><td>Limited Omniscient</td><td></td><td>Restricted to Participation</td></tr>
<tr><td>Perspective:</td><td>Omnipresent Overview</td><td></td><td>Restricted to Participation</td></tr>
</table>

PERSON

FIRST: This is the narrative voice which refers to itself and speaks directly to the reader.

FIRST SINGULAR: The narrative voice, in its capacity as story teller, refers to itself as an individual and not as part of a group by the use of the word *I*.

FIRST PLURAL: The narrative voice, speaking to the reader as an individual, constantly refers to itself as part of a group, using *we*.

THIRD SINGULAR: The narrative voice refers to one character at a time and talks about groups of people only in the sense of them being observed by one individual: *He saw the* flag. *She saw the* people dancing.

THIRD PLURAL: The narrative voice always talks about a group of two or more people, using *they* or *them*.

TENSE

PAST: The narrative voice talks about things which occurred in the past.

PRESENT: The narrative voice refers to actions as if they're happening at the time they're being told about.

FUTURE: The narrative voice tells about things which will happen in the future.

ATTITUDE

OBJECTIVE: This voice shows no emotional involvement in the actions in the narration. It seems to have no attitude about the characters or what they do, and assumes almost a scientific objectivity about the events.

SUBJECTIVE: This voice cares about the characters and what they do and lets the reader know this by making comments indicating it has made value judgements.

INVOLVEMENT

**PART OF
ACTION:** The narrative voice is one of the characters who takes a part in the events in either a main or supporting role.

OBSERVER: The narrative voice watches the action from some removed vantage point. It is never a participator, rather a viewer of events.

KNOWLEDGE

**LIMITED
OMNISCIENT:** This voice has a wide range of possibilities. It can be in more than one mind and know what is happening in many places. It has an expanded view of the action.

**RESTRICTED TO
OBSERVATION:** This voice has a narrow view, as if it had knowledge gained by watching the action in the house next door.

**RESTRICTED TO
PARTICIPATION:** The narrative voice is part of the action and can't know what is happening in other places, nor can it know what happens to other characters when it is not with them.

PERSPECTIVE

**OMNIPRESENT
OVERVIEW:** The narrative voice must have some form of omniscience, for it can describe things in two places at one time and take the reader into the past and future and can show the reader the actions from any angle or from any vantage point it chooses.

**RESTRICTED TO
PERSONAL
VIEW:** The narrative voice assumes the position of a person in the story either as a participant or an observer. This view is limited to what a real person could see, hear and know. On the next page are some examples of these points of view.

PERSON: First and Third, Singular and Plural:

First person singular: I *saw* the dog Third person singular: *He saw* the dog.

First person plural: *We saw* the dog. Third person plural: *They saw* the dog.

TENSE: Past - Present - Future:

First singular, past: *I saw* the dog. Third plural, past: *They saw* the dog.

First singular, present: *I see* the dog.

Third plural, present: *They* see the dog

First singular, future: *I will see* the dog. Third plural, future - *They will see* the dog.

ATTITUDE: Objective - Subjective:

First person, singular, past, objective: I saw *the hungry dog* (Note that the narrative voice gives no indication of how it feels about seeing a hungry animal.)

Third person plural, future, subjective: They will see *the poor hungry dog.*

INVOLVEMENT: Part of action (central or peripheral), Observer (minimal or non-involved)

First person, singular, past, subjective, central to action: *I felt sorry* for the *poor, hungry dog* when I *had to chase it away* from the door.

Third person, singular, past, objective, non-involved: *He watched the cook chase* the hungry dog away from the kitchen doorway.

First person, plural, past, subjective, minimally involved: *We held the door so* the cook could chase away the *poor, hungry dog.*

KNOWLEDGE: Limited omniscient, restricted to participation and restricted to observation:

Third person, past, subjective, non-involved, observer, limited omniscient: It *was a cruel thing* that the *boys* should have to hold the door *when they felt so sorry* for the *lonely* and hungry dog that the cook, *who really hated all animals,* chased away from the back of the trash-filled alley.

First person, present, objective, minimally involved, knowledge restricted to action: *Opening the door for the cook, I* see the hungry dog and *watch through the crack in the hinge line* as the cook throws a rock and chases it away.

First person plural, past, subjective, non-involved, knowledge restricted to observation: *From our room over the alley we looked down on the back of the restaurant* and there saw the two boys hold the door for the *cruel cook* so he could throw stones at the *poor dog*.

PERSPECTIVE: omnipresent overview and limited to personal view

Third person, past, objective, non-involved, limited omniscient, omnipresent overview: *The dog had been in the alley happily rooting in the garbage only a short time* when the two *not-very-bright boys* opened the door, and the cook, *who never had liked dogs*, threw stones, and the frightened dog ran down to the corner and into the alley in the next block where it found better pickings anyway.

First person, plural, present, objective, restricted to observation, limited to personal view: By *leaning over the sill* and looking down, *we can see* the door opening and *someone* throwing stones and then the door shots and the alley is empty again.

There is a lot of material here, but it must be learned by all writers. It is not essential that you memorize the labels for all of the choices you might make for your narrative voice, but they must be well chosen by you, and you should be consistent in their use. You can see the problem that it would cause, if, in one part of your narrative, you were to have the narrative voice know what a character is thinking, and in another part, you were to write as if your narrative voice had no idea what that character is thinking.

It'll help you if you practice controlling the positions of your narrative voices. The following exercise will help you do this.

Cheerleader

Using six different of point of view conditions, write six 150 to 200 word descriptive pieces. Write about a cheerleader at a sports event using the following narrative voices:

1. The cheerleader herself
2. Her mother
3. Two older men in the stands
4. Her boyfriend
5. An older lady
6. An objective voice

An example of how to set up your narrative voices should help:

When you write using each of the voices, you should list at the top of the page the conditions of your narrative voice like this:

> *Point of view - first person, present tense, subjective, involved, knowledge limited to participation, perspective limited to personal view.*

5

Truth in the Narrative Voice

One of the problems readers have is knowing who to believe. This is not too difficult if they understand the nature of the narrative voice talking to them. Fiction consists of a story teller relating a series of events, and the complications of belief are fewer than are found in our everyday lives. As a writer, you must appreciate the confusion that a reader is subject to.

When we're told by our families and friends of things that have happened, we understand that the events are clouded by the limitations of memory and the quite natural desire of the story tellers to make the stories interesting to us and to put the best light possible on their own involvement. This is not offensive to us because it has become a convention of interaction. We find this condition when we read. We must accept that in some narrative voice situations we must not take what we're told as the literal truth.

In fiction, there are two kinds of truth and two levels for them. The first truth is that which we have come to accept as defining the genre (the kind of fiction we're reading). The narrator sets the limits for our disbelief, and we accept what happens in fantasy as realistic (within the limits of our imagination) so that we may enjoy the stories, as we accept science fiction, historical romance and westerns or any other "unrealistic" situations. This kind of truth we agree to when we decide to read in these genres, and this does not give us a problem with believability, for we suspend our disbelief to enjoy the reading.

So, we have the two kinds of truth we must deal with in fiction, that kind which sets the genre and establishes the conventions of our belief, and the kind which is set by the limits of our ability to accept what is told us.

An example of this second kind of truth violation is found in *Relentless,* an adventure novel by Brian Garfield. The hero is in a line shack far up in the mountains in the remote northwest part of this country, in the winter, in a snowstorm. The shack has no electricity and of course no running water. It is just a shack to be used if ranch hands are caught in a blizzard. In the middle of a tense scene with some bank robbers, Garfield gives us this line: "He flushed the toilet but the noise was almost obscured by the steady roar of the blizzard against the log walls."

At this point Garfield lost me. We accept as a convention of the adventure genre that the hero would not be "realistic"—he'd be bigger than life, the bad guys would be super-bad, the women would be virtuous, there would be cliff-hanging scenes, there would be time pressures on the hero, and the hero would be misunderstood and not appreciated by the conventional law enforcement agencies. This is all part of the genre, but we cannot accept flushing a toilet in a mountain cabin in winter when there is no water or electricity.

Garfield does this because he has to get one of the men out of the room, and at the same time he has to keep all of the characters in the cabin. But, there must have been some other way to do that without violating what the reader would accept as "true."

Within this kind of truth there are two levels that we have grown to understand and accept. One level is the truth of the narrative voice when the narrator is objective and is non-involved in the story as a character. This is fiction's most common narrative voice. If this voice tells us that Betty is beautiful, we believe it, because we know that the voice comes from a mind which does not love Betty and has no ego involvement in her beauty.

The other level of truth is that version given us by a narrative voice which assumes a character role. In this situation, we respond much as we do when we're told stories by our friends when they were a part of the action. To be polite, we pretend to believe what they tell us, but we reserve judgment until there is some verification from another party. We know if our friend, John, tells us that his new girlfriend, Betty, is beautiful, she may be, but we accept that this is his judgment, and it is not an objective truth. He's not describing her appearance as a non-involved narrator would, but is telling us how he sees her.

We must understand that the narrative voice in fiction, which assumes the role of a character, speaks subjectively. All that the voice tells us is suspect. The character's voice is not stating a reality, it's relating an event as it was seen, clouded by wishes, anxieties, ego involvement and desires to impress us.

It would help you to understand an author's expectations of the narrative voice believability and the limitation a reader must place on the believability of a narrative voice if you write a creative piece which demonstrates these two levels of truth.

An exercise which will help you to understand this is to relate an incident from your life. This should be one in which there was a good deal of tension involving you and other members of your family. There can be peripheral characters if you need them— characters not central to the story line. This short narration will be easiest in past tense and should have three narrative voices, each telling a part of the "true" story as it is understood by that voice.

1. Character A - First person, subjective, involved, limited in knowledge
2. Character B - First person, subjective, involved, limited in knowledge
3. Narrative voice C - Non-character, third person, objective, non-involved, limited omniscient

The three voices will speak to the reader and will relate a part of the same event but will be handicapped or liberated by the nature of their involvement. You, as author, of course, will write all three positions, but the narrative voice, as first person participant, will assume the position in the story of either character A or B as prejudiced by being involved, but you will present the "truth" of the account as given by narrative voice C.

You will have to plan the mechanics of the narration so your reader will be able to understand who's speaking. Any way you can do this to make it clear to your reader is fine. Try not to set your piece up as a play. The easiest voice to differentiate will be that of C, because of the difference in the point of view (third person).

You can make the voices of A and B recognizable by creating differences in their:
1. Attitude
2. Sex
3. Vocabulary
4. Sentence length and type
5. Activities
6. Tone

An easy way to set your piece up would be to have the objective narrative voice be C, and then to have C call on the other two voices to speak. The model is not done this way. This example may not be the best way to do this exercise, and if it doesn't work for you, invent your own mechanics.

Note the labels in the following model: (A), (B), and (C), indicating which narrative voice is speaking. It's labeled for you to understand who's speaking and how the "reality" of that voice influences the story.

(C) There was a good bit of trouble at 231 Oak Street last week. It ended with the police coming and parking their car with its flashing red light casting its intermittent glow off the windows all along the street. Before it was over, most of the neighbors were standing in their bathrobes in front of their houses wondering what in the world was going on. Mrs. Wiggins is still convinced it had something to do with spies. Of course, she has always looked for communists ever since her TV got the rollover problem during the McCarthy hearings. That was when Ralph's TV Repair still used the red truck. "There has to be a reason for this," she was fond of saying. The first indication the neighbors had that there might be a problem was when the first gunshot was heard.

(A) I'd been trying to tell my dad all summer that there was something in the wall of my room. Late at night, after the house got quiet, I could hear small scratching noises. Lots of times I'd get up and turn on the lights. But, of course, I could never see anything, and no one would believe me. Dad always told me it was my imagination. Uncle Henry used to hear it after he came to

live with us. That was after Aunt Eunice died, and he took to drinking so much beer all the time. Dad never believed him even when he was sober. Dad used to say, "Henry's been hearing things all his life. Don't you start." It used to make me furious when he didn't believe me and told me it was my growing imagination. Where does it say that just because a person's only twelve years old she's not supposed to know what she hears?

(B) I have a business in this town and a reputation to maintain. What happened last week wasn't my fault. If I didn't have so many people living in my house, I know it never would have happened. Janice was always hearing something in the walls. I used to tell her it was her imagination, but I thought it was probably mice and didn't want to scare her. And my wife's drunk brother should never be allowed out in public. He's a real danger to himself and all the rest of us. I told him not to bring that gun with him when he came to visit, but no, he wouldn't listen.

(C) There were at least six calls to the police station. Down there they thought there must have been a small war going on with all the reports of "Shots heard." They hadn't been at the house but a few minutes when the new emergency truck, the one the village just bought, came racing around the corner and smashed into the back of the only police car the village owns. Ralph Venter lost his job over that.

(A) Gosh, it would have been all right if Uncle Henry hadn't been still up when I first saw the bat. I think the trouble all really started when I ran through the living room in my pajamas shouting, "Help! He's in my room!" Uncle Henry was well into the TV and beer by then. Mom and Dad had been in bed for at least an hour. He didn't know I meant that I had finally seen the cause of the noises. A bat had landed on the end of my bed. I could see it in the light from the streetlight which came in the front window of my room. I was running to get my tennis racket. Uncle Henry must have thought there was a man in my room.

(B) I first woke up when Henry yelled. Betty and I were asleep in the back room, and I heard him yell, "You stay there. I'll get the gun!" I grabbed an old six iron from the upstairs hall closet and ran toward Janice's room ready to defend her against I didn't know what. I had just turned the corner in the dark hall when Henry hit the top of the stairs. I could hear Janice yelling now, and I admit there was a good bit of confusion. I think the head of the six iron connected with Henry's nose. I think that's how it got broken. Anyway, that's when the gun went off the first time. The shot went out through the side of our house and clear through the wall next door and into the front of Old Lady Wigeon's TV:

25

(C) At the first shot, which blew up the television next door, Mr. Bancroft, a retired bank guard, thought there must be a robber in the neighborhood and got his shotgun out of the basement. He was the one who shot out the headlights on the volunteer fire truck, that was the one that ended up on his porch. Clint Williams said he never would have hit the house if he hadn't been trying to avoid the kid running down the driveway waving the tennis racket.

(A) I think it was after the first shot that Dad's golf club went through the hall window and onto the front lawn. I'll just bet it hit Minster's dog, and that's why it acted so strange and got reported as "A Mad Rabid Beast Loose in the Neighborhood" by Mrs. Willis who was walking her cat by the front of our house. If it hadn't been for her, I'll bet the animal protection man would never have broken Uncle Henry's glasses with the net. Anyway, after the gun went off the first time, and Dad and Uncle Henry fell down the stairs on top of me, and the gun bounced down and went off the second time and put a hole in the power transformer that gave power to the whole neighborhood. . .

Of course, this never happened at my house. I was just having fun with the story line. You should recognize my copy of the style of James Thurber in this short example. If you don't, you might get some of his work from the library and try him. He's really very funny.

6

Dramatic Dialogue

One of the more difficult tasks a writer has is to make his characters sound like real people when they talk together. This is hard, because when people talk, they use so much facial expression, body language and voice inflection that help to convey meaning that just their words do not mean nearly as much by themselves. As an example of this, examine the following dialogue, which is a fairly realistic representation of how people talk to each other:

The man comes in the kitchen door. His wife is doing dishes.

She: Did you get it?
He: No.
She: Now what?
He: You got me. I don't have any answers.
She: What did they say?
He: "No."
She: And?
He: Don't ask me.
She: What a mess!

Even though this is the way people really talk, it doesn't mean much to readers unless they know what's going on. This is called realistic dialogue. Look now at pedantic dialogue, that type found in some books for children, in which all the information readers might need to know is included. In fact, often there's so much information given that, as you will see, this type of dialogue slows the action down so much that the movement toward the ending of the story is too slow for readers to tolerate.

The same scene.

*He: Hello, Betty, my wife of 23 years. I'm back from the bank where I asked for a loan
      to buy our son's first car.*
She: Did the bank loan us the money?
He: The banker said we've borrowed all the money we can on my income.
*She: What can we do now that we can't get the money? It is John's 16th birthday in
      one week, and we promised him that we would help him buy a car.*
He: I don't know what we can do. You will have to tell him we can't get the money.

27

She: You should help me tell him. He's not just my son, you know. He belongs to both of us. We both have to tell him.

Somewhere between these two extremes lies acceptable dialogue. It's impossible to tell a young writer how to write dialogue except to suggest reading good writers. You should look at Hemingway's short stories. He's particularly good at dialogue. His *Hills Like White Elephants is* a good example of dialogue as close to realistic as you might want to get. Also, John Gardner's *Nickel Mountain* will give you some examples of excellent dialogue.

Since fiction is telling about conflict, dialogue must help the movement of the story to a resolution. It has, of course, other functions. When we see characters talking, it helps us understand character relationships, motivations, personalities and backgrounds.

A good way to practice creating just the words of dialogue is to write as if for plays. For this exercise you will write a dialogue which will be in play form but will be written as if it were only a small part of a much longer work. One of the two characters must represent a protagonist force and the other must represent an antagonist force.

So that your reader will know where the dialogue takes place, you should introduce the action with a set description like the ones found in the beginnings of plays. If you're not familiar with this, look up some plays.

You'll have to give motivations to both characters, because, unless it's clear in your mind exactly what both of them want, their actions will not be understood by your reader, so after reading only one or two pages of your dialogue, your reader should be able to tell what motivates each character.

The set description and the character directions (author directions for actions and descriptions of speech) should be in present tense. Note the following example:

It is the first day of summer vacation for John, a high school junior. He is in his room in a typical middle class home. There are the usual rock star posters and school pennants hung on the walls. His mother enters.

Mother: *John, now that summer's here, there are some things we have to get straight. (She sits on the edge of his bed.)*

John: *(Sitting up) Sure, Mom, but do we have to talk about it now? It's only ten o'clock.*

An experienced author might do most of his outlining in his head, but you might benefit from writing your ideas in notes like the following.

1. Forces in conflict:
   A. Protagonist: _____

   B. Antagonist: _____

2. Characters in conflict:

   A. _____

   B. _____

3. The major characteristics of the two characters:

   A. _____

   _____

   _____

   B. _____

   _____

   _____

4. The nature of the conflict:

   _____

   _____

   _____

   _____

7. The speech patterns of the characters:

   A. Antagonist: Diction: _____

   Example: _____

Sentence Length:_____ Example: _____

_____

_____

B. Protagonist: Diction: _____

Example: _____

Sentence Length:_____

Example: _____

8. The attitudes of the characters to the situation and to each other.
   A. Antagonist at the:
   Opening: _____

   Confrontation: _____

   Climax: _____

   B. Protagonist at the:
       Opening: _____

   Confrontation: _____

   Climax: _____

7

Reader Reactions

You've read a number of times now of the importance of controlling the emotions of your readers. You'll learn with this exercise that this isn't a hard thing to do. You must know who your readership is and then a decision must be made as to what procedures would be most effective in this effort to control. To demonstrate to you that this can be done, I've selected one emotional reaction, shock, and will show you how readers can be shocked. Once your readership has been identified, and you desire to create and then control reactions to what you write, you'll be successful if you analyze what your readers are feeling prior to your period of manipulation attempt and then make the decision about what would be needed to have them move to some new emotional position. This exercise demonstrates this process.

Shock was chosen because it's an easy emotional reaction to create. It's a rude insult to the sensibilities of readers and is characterized by surprise. For this exercise you can, in about 1000 words, shock your readers if you follow these steps:

1. You should create a character with whom your readers can identify. The potential for shock will be greater if your character is innocent. The conventions for innocence in the middle class in this country suggest that the character should be young. The young are thought of as more innocent than are adults, and if the character is prepubescent, he/she will be seen as even more innocent. If you want to use an adult, the character should be at least seventy years old. There is an innocent and non-threatening quality to the elderly.

    Girls are thought of as more innocent than boys, blondes as more innocent than dark haired people, and sheltered children as more innocent than are children who have had varied experiences. If you choose to use animals, you should use an herbivore instead of a carnivore, for rabbits are seen as more innocent than foxes.

    Your readers should get to know your character fairly well. They should see him/her react to other people and hear him/her in conversation.

2. Once your readers have identified with your character, you should put the character in a situation which is life threatening. Your readers should be sure there is no way the character can survive.

3. You should release the character from the threat. This must be done in such a way that your readers will believe it could happen naturally and not be a contrived release. This will put your readers in a relaxed mood. They'll be tense from reading of the threatening situation the character is in, and when the character is released from danger, they'll let their defenses down. It is at this point your readers will be most vulnerable to manipulation and will be ready to be shocked.

4. Anything that now happens to your character which is truly bad will shock your readers. This must be done suddenly and it must not take more than a sentence or two. Very little time should pass between the release of the character from the threatening situation and that event which is destructive.

The force or action which is bad for or destroys the character should, in some way, be related to the threatening situation, but it should be of such a nature that your readers could not anticipate it happening, and it must not be foreshadowed. This exercise can end at the point at which the character is damaged. Lingering diseases and brain tumors are terrible deaths but are not shocking because of the length of time it takes the victim to die. I know that this doesn't sound pleasant, but then shock isn't a pleasant experience. You cannot learn to write if you concentrate on just pleasant experiences.

You may test the effectiveness of your writing by having a few people read your piece of narration. The readers you select should be in the group you designated as your readership when you designed the narration. Before having your paper read, you might decide what questions you will ask your readers. You will want to know if they were sure if the character would die during the life threatening situation, whether they felt relief when the character was released from threat, and finally, if they were shocked at the damage or destruction of the character.

It might be easier if you make some notes before you begin to write. I'd make the following were I to do this exercise:

Shock Notes

1. The characteristics of the innocent character:

_____

_____

2. Why the reader should identify with this character:

_____

_____

_____

3. The life-threatening situation: _____

_____

4. Method of character release from threat:

_____

_____

_____

5. Method of the damage or destruction of the character:

_____

_____

_____

8

Symbols in Literature

In literature, symbols are an effective but subtle way to convey information. Symbols are concrete objects that are made to represent, or that can represent, abstract concepts. It would be a very complicated job for a writer to write about one of his characters having feelings of patriotism, but it would be easy for the writer to have his character stop and look up at the American flag.

As an example, suppose a man and a woman have just seen their son off on the bus. This is the first time he has ever been off the farm and they love him and will miss him. He has been called to the army. The author could tell the reader that the parents are proud of their son and are glad that he can serve his country as his father and grandfather had. He could have them discuss this. But, this might be cumbersome and get in the way of the progress of the story.

This is where a symbol can help. The parents can stand and watch the bus leave on the county road out of town, then turn and walk toward their car which is parked in front of the post office. Just before they get in the car, the man can look up to the flag flying over the post office building. He then can look over to his wife and see that she too is looking at the flag. The man can give a short nod, and the woman can smile at him, and they can step into the car.

In this case the reader is given the feeling that they're proud that their son has gone off to war without the author having to say so.

Our lives are full of symbols. The red on the stop sign, the cigarette with a line through it, company logos, the signs along country roads with deer on them, the yellow of school busses and these marks on this page are all symbols. Our lives would be much more complicated without them.

In fiction, symbols are used to give readers feelings about events and objects in a way that no amount of descriptive writing could. In order for symbols to be effective, the creator and the reader must have understandings in common. For example, many of the symbols in Asian writing have no value for Western readers because the Eastern writer and Western reader have no common cultural base. Therefore your choice of symbols will depend on who you select as your audience. You'd use different ones for adult readers than you'd use for children. This is one of the reasons you always should establish your readership before you begin writing. You will write a short narrative. Its outline has been designed to allow you to use as many symbols as you can. It will not be good writing, because there will be too many symbols in it, but it will give you a good feeling for how they work. Use the scenario below.

Scenario

Two young farm boys, after eating breakfast, ask to go to the woods to pick berries. Whey are warned about crossing the creek but they do so. They become lost on the far side of the creek and have to spend the night in the woods. The next morning they find their way home.

Symbols
1. Home (this involves):
    A. Light
    B. Warmth
    C. Food
    D. Love and kindness
    E. Care
    F. Kitchen and cooking
    G. Mother (her symbols are)
        1) Apron
        2) Flour on face
        3) Work at sink and stove
        4) Security and love
    H. Apple or berry pie

2. Creek (banks smooth on the home side, rough on the far side)
    A. Swamp
    B. Darkness
    C. Wet ground
    D. Bushes that cling

3. Night (darkness)
    A. Tall trees that threaten
    B. Night animals (sounds)
    C. Storms
    D. Lack of stars and moon

4. Dawn
    A. Light in the east
    B. Light in the window of the farmhouse
    C. Smell of breakfast cooking
    D. Sounds of home.

One way to start this narrative would be to separate the positive symbols from the negative (those concrete objects and images that give us good feelings from those that make us feel insecure). One way to do this is to have the positive symbols be on the home side of the creek and the negative ones on the far side. The symbols can be used in the narrative voice description of events and the places and in the dialogue between the boys and between the boys and their mother. A problem you will have to solve is one of logic. Why don't the mother and father come out looking for the two boys when they don't return home?

9

Identification and Symbolism
in an
Extended Flashback

You should be able to combine in one piece of fiction some of the skills you have practiced. They work in combination in the same ways they work by themselves; the only difference is you will have to keep a number of things in mind at the same time. In this exercise you will be writing a piece of fiction in which you will shift from the past tense to a prior time and then back again to the time frame you were originally in. You will create a symbol which will work to help your reader appreciate the story, create characters with whom your readers will identify and put your characters in such a situation that your readers will empathize with them.

Scenario

Mr. and Mrs. Smith are packing the last of their son's toys and putting them in the trunk of their car. This is the last step before they leave their home. They are moving away because they cannot stand the pain of living any longer in this house where their son was killed. The rest of the house is empty. As Mrs. Smith is putting a box in the trunk, she looks up and sees the broken kite (the symbol) hanging in a large tree in the front yard. This makes her think of the day Billy was killed climbing the tree to get down his kite. (The narrative voice tells the reader the mother's memories of that day. The transition is accomplished by two or three uses of the past perfect tense. The rest of the flashback portion of the narrative, her memory, is given in straight past tense.) After her recollection of that unfortunate day, she shuts the trunk and she and her husband drive away.

FLASHBACK:

The use of the past perfect tense indicates to your reader that an event is being recounted that has taken place prior to the current time being talked about by the narrative voice. This works this way no matter what tense the narrative voice is using for the rest of the story. The chart below may make this clearer. An example might also help:

Mrs. Jones lifted the trunk lid of her car and glanced up to the large tree near the road. Most of the leaves were down now, and she could clearly see the broken sticks and the rain-soaked and sun-faded paper streamers of Billy's kite. It had been so colorful and now was pale and shattered.

Through a mist of tears, she again saw her young son running in the door with his birthday present and hear his high-pitched voice yelling, "We got it, Mom. We got big blue one."

(now the flashback)

It had been Billy's eighth birthday and he had been promised the kite in the window of Jenson's hardware store. Billy had talked about little else. . .

When you're ready to bring your readers out of your flashback, you should pick up the action at the same place where you leave to start the flashback. In the model above, I interrupt the story line at the point where Mrs. Jones lifts the lid of the car trunk. After the events shown in the flashback, I must take my readers back to the story line and pick up the action at the same place. This will keep my readers from becoming confused about where they are in the story. I'll shift my readers from the earlier situation to the narrative now (see below) by starting a new paragraph and by having Mrs. Jones do a continuation of the thing she was doing when I broke away to go into the past to explain the death of the boy.

Mrs. Jones dropped the last box of toys in the full trunk and slammed the lid. Sound was muffled in the rain-heavy air. She turned and called to John, but her voice was a croak and caught in her throat. She realized she had been crying and wiped the rain and tears from her face. "John," she yelled, "are you ready to leave yet?"

Using a Flashback

The time frame as the narrative
voice is telling the story

Past >-----------------------------Narrative now-------------------------------> Future

Past perfect	Past tense	Future tense
Any acts here must use *had*.	(He went)	(He will go)
(He had gone.)		

38

The time frame of the telling of the story by the narrative voice is referred to as *The narrative now*. This can be in any tense you care to use, the flashback will work just the same. In this exercise you will have your narrative voice use past tense.

It is a convention of narration that when authors wants to show readers something that has happened prior to the time when the action of the story is taking place, they have their narrative voices use the past perfect tense two or three times and then shift back into the previously used tense form. Readers understand this and accept the two or three uses of the past perfect tense as a transitional device to get them into an earlier time frame, and they'll stay with the narrator in that earlier time frame until such time as the narrative voice indicates a shift back into the main time frame of the story. If this doesn't make sense, read that passage again. You must understand the mechanics of this to do this exercise. If it still isn't clear, read it again.

It will be much easier for you to make the shift into and out of past events if you keep in mind that there should be no time lapse in the story line at the shifts. The break into a prior time to show some contributing or explanatory event and back again should be clean cuts, where the character or the narrative voice (whichever mind is used for the transition) continues with the activity engaged in when the breaks occur.

This may sound confusing, as many new things do, but it is not at all complicated, and once you see it done in the model, it will be very clear how this works.

SYMBOLISM

Of course, you remember that literary symbolism is the use of concrete objects to represent abstract concepts.

In order for the kite in this narration to be an effective symbol for the boy and for the dreams his parents have for him, the kite and the boy both must be described as having some of the same characteristics. You might even use some of the same words and phrases in describing them.

Example #1:

Kite

> *The kite he had picked out was the brightest one in the store, and he was sure it would fly higher than any of the kites the other kids had. His kite really had a future; he could tell. When he bent the slender, white wooden sticks, made to stretch the paper on, he could almost feel the strength of the. . .*

Boy

On the top of the last box he carried was the really good microscope they had given Joey for his eighth birthday. When he got to the back of the car, he said softly to his wife, "What should we do with this? We can't just dump it in the boxes with the rest of this stuff. It cost over a hundred dollars.

"There must be another future doctor out there somewhere who would just love to have it," she said, as she reached out and touched the smooth, cold metal.

Example # 2:

The boy and the kite both fall from the tree. They are both destroyed as a result of being in the tree.

The dreams the boy has for the kite and the dreams the parents have for the boy are similar. They're both seen as beautiful and capable of doing wonderful things.

IDENTIFICATION

Fictional characters can be created so as to encourage reader identification in three ways:
1. The character can be created to *be like the intended reade*r.
2. The character can be created in such a way that the intended reader would *like to be like* the character.
3. The character can be created in such detail that the reader *can understand what motivates* the character and thus appreciate the character's actions.

The characters to be identified with by your reader are the parents of the boy who dies.

EMPATHY

This is the feeling readers have for a character with whom they identify, one who is experiencing pain or pleasure.

In order for any situation to produce an empathetic reaction in readers, the readers must first have identified with the characters, so the writer must spend some time developing them. In this exercise, the readers should witness the parents interact with compassion and tenderness as they share pain at the loss of their son.

In the following excerpt from a student's writing, an intelligent adult would have an easy time identifying with the parents. The author created the man and woman as intelligent and sensitive people who obviously care for each other. They're cooperating in the job of moving the last of their things out of the house.

"Phil, while I put these things in the trunk, could you close all the windows?"
"Sure, honey," answered Phil.

They both work at giving Joey the love and attention he needs.

. . .he had come running into the house after school, talking excitedly about Ben's newest toy.

Joey's father had taken him to the toy store that evening, and upon returning home, Joey proudly showed off his kite. "See, Mommy, we got the last blue one they had. Isn't it neat, huh, isn't it neat?"
"Let's put it together now," said his father, "and maybe we can fly it tomorrow."

The parents together suffer the pain of Joey's death.

Phil put his arm around Lynn, and tears ran down her face as. . .
"Phil, Phil, our baby is gone," sobbed Lynn.
"I know, Honey, I know. "
"But, why him? Why him?"

I can almost hear you thinking "What do I do now?" I'd suggest that you re-read the scenario and then make some notes. It would be a good idea to make lists of the characteristics of the kite and the boy that are similar. It would be easiest for you to put these side by side so as to make the parallels more obvious. Then, as you write, you can refer to the lists to make sure you use the similarities. This will ensure that your reader will appreciate the kite as a symbol for the boy.

You should identify who your readers will be so as to be able to make a decision about the method you will use for the creation of your characters so your readers will identify with them.

You might also list the elements of your narrative voice. If you are not sure you remember all of them, check back to the section on narrative voice options.

This exercise is fairly complicated, but, by working your way through it, you will gain a good bit of experience.

10

Creating Mood

Since the consideration of the feelings of the reader is such an important aspect of good writing, you need much practice creating emotional reactions in your readers. One of the conditions you will need to learn to control is the moods of your readers. This involves not only establishing the moods but the control of your readers to the extent that you can change the moods they experience.

In this exercise you'll write a short story in which you'll produce three distinct moods in your readers. Use the following scenario.

A young woman living in the city feels the need to escape for a few days from a bad situation. She drives to the deserted home of her deceased grandparents. This is the place where she had spent many happy times as a child. The house sits on a finger of land surrounded by water and swamp. There is an old bridge which is used to cross a creek which separates the property from the country road. The nearest neighbor lives at least a mile away.

When she gets to the house, she finds it in disrepair. There is no electricity, but a rusty hand pump does work. A sudden fall storm washes away the old bridge, stranding her on what has become an island. The reader sees through her eyes and hears through her ears what the character thinks are the nightly attempts of some creature to gain entrance.

At first it is only a scraping at the windows; it could be the bushes that have grown high at the sides of the house. Later, during the first night, she hears around the doors, sniffing sounds, like a large dog might make. As the night grows older, the sounds get louder and the sniffing is now around the tops of the doors. At one time that night, she sees a great furry body press against the window in the parlor. The next day she can find no evidence of any large animal.

The second night she can hear scratching against the front door. The sniffing has become grunting and snorting and is much louder. She stands by the door and can feel it press in and can hear what she thinks are claws that tear the wood. She retreats to the upstairs bedroom and there sees a furry body against the window on the second floor. She feels the old house shudder as it leans away from the weight that presses against it.

The next morning, the sheriff, looking for flood damage, sees her car in front of the house and investigates. He finds her in the closet curled into a fetal position. She'll not speak or acknowledge his presence. The narrative is finished when he carries her out of the house to his boat.

The readers are not told by the narrative voice that there is a large animal. If the narrative voice says it is there, then it really must be there. The readers are not told by the narrative voice that the door is damaged. The sheriff can look at the door, can even run his hand over the wood, but the readers can not know what the sheriff thinks. The sheriff is alone, and the narrative voice does not get into his mind.

The mood in your story will be established by controlling the following factors:
1. Setting
2. Character attitude toward place, situation, and other characters
3. Prior events
4. Colors and patterns
5. The orientation and size of structures
6. Lights and shadows
7. Sentence length and variety
8. Word choice
9. Movement
10. Dialogue
11. Narrator attitude

You are to create three moods:
1. In the first part of the story, your readers must feel just as the woman does—confined and frustrated by being trapped in the city. The readers should be released from this mood when the character gets to the highway and is in the countryside.
2. Your readers should feel joy and security when the woman arrives at the old house.
3. Your reader should feel terror as the woman is beset by the large animal. . . or by her imagination.

MOOD CREATING FACTORS

SETTING:
There will be three settings in this narrative:
1. The city (first in her apartment then in her car)
2. The country roads (first the highway and then the open country spaces)
3. The old house

CHARACTER ATTITUDE TOWARD THE LOCALE AND THE SITUATION:
1. In the city she feels confined and trapped by the tall buildings and her own loneliness.
2. On the country roads she feels free for the first time.
3. At the farm she feels secure and then feels as if she's under siege.

PRIOR EVENTS:
1. The narrative voice, directly or through the character's remembered conversations, tells the reader what has happened to the character which makes her want to leave the city.

2. The character remembers back to when she was a girl when the people and events were good for her and to her.

COLORS AND PATTERNS:
1. The city is gray and dirty, and she must live in constant shadow, with the tall buildings looming over her.
2. When on the country roads, she can see for some distance the rolling hills and the sun on the grass and trees.
3. At the edge of her grandparents' property, the rising water in the river threatens the bridge.
4. The fog covers the farm and closes in her world.
5. It is fall, most of the leaves are off the trees and the colors are gray and brown.
6. The house is old, the siding boards are loose and twisted, the porch sags, the roof droops, and the colors in the house are muted with fading and dust.

ORIENTATION AND SIZE OF STRUCTURES:

1. In her apartment, the character can feel shut in by the tall buildings that hang over her, blocking out the sun for most of the day.
2. In her car, she can feel trapped by the other cars and trucks, and the stop lights can all be red when she gets to them on the streets which are narrow and clogged .
3   On the highway out of town, the trucks will be much larger than her car and loom over her and can be moving very fast, and a monster truck can even ride her rear bumper, making her drive faster than she feels is safe.
4. At the farm, the bridge can be narrow, and the road can be muddy and rutted.
5. The house can be tall, and the windows can look like sightless eyes.
6. The stairs to the upper level can be narrow and uneven.

LIGHT AND SHADOW:

1. The sun is dim behind mist and clouds.
2. The nights can be very dark, the moon can be hidden behind clouds, and the stars might not be visible.
3. There might not be electricity, and then the oil lamps could give a yellow glow to the house and the yard and cast long feeble shadows.
4. The fireplace might throw wavering shadows and images on the walls and ceiling.
5. Her flashlight could be growing weak, and its yellowing beam could barely light the stairway.
6. The oil lamp, when she goes out to the car at night and when she goes upstairs, can cast her shadow behind her, and its huge image can follow her through the darkness of the yard and the house.

MOVEMENT:

1. The wind can make the trees and bushes scrape and claw at the siding and windows.
2. The clouds, at first, might race darkly over the house and property and then hang heavy and low over the swamp and the land the farm is on.
3. The water in the river must rise and wash the bridge away and continue to rise toward the house, and her island could grow smaller each hour.
4. The old house can creak and moan in the wind and seem to her to lean into the gusts.
5. The bridge must be out, there is no telephone, she cannot cross the river and there are no neighbors. There is no movement to be seen during the day except maybe a lone hawk, which could circle endlessly against the gray sky. At night, the only movement might be the sounds of mice or rats in the walls, the bushes scratching on the siding and windows, and the fur that rubs against the windows, higher and higher each time she sees it.

DIALOGUE:

1. You might let your readers know how troubled the character is by having some dialogue going on in her mind—she could be talking to her ex-husband, her deceased grandparents or some friend from her past.
2. When she gets to the house, she might remember conversations she has had with other members of her family when they were all together.
3. She might talk to herself, at first with a sense of relief at being alone and away from her troubles, but later she might try to explain to herself the strange snuffling and rubbing at the doors and the sounds of the fur against the glass.

NARRATIVE VOICE ATTITUDE:

1. The narrator must be objective—so as not to seem sympathetic, increasing your readers' empathetic attitudes and making your job of creating mood easier.
2. The creation of the second mood, release, can be accomplished only if your readers are aware of what the prior conditions were—the girl must be seen as being released from something, for she has been living in the city and has gone through a bad time.

SYMBOLS:

The city can be used to symbolize her feelings of being trapped and increase her feelings of despair. The buildings are tall and shut out the light. The air is dirty. The streets are narrow and lined with trash. The traffic is slow and the air is hot and full of exhaust.

The sun is hidden by clouds and smog. The highway out of town is full of large trucks (their tires are taller than her small compact), but the sun is shining and she can drive faster now. The countryside opens up her view of the landscape. The sun is bright, the air is fresh. There are trees and birds. She's free!

Water or a river is an effective symbol for going from one place or situation to another. She leaves behind her the problems of the city and/or her failed marriage. She can see in the distance the home which will be her sanctuary. A house is a symbol of security and love.

The old house is surrounded by overgrown weeds and bushes. The shutters are loose, the boards are warped and the paint is flaking off. Her memory of the house is romantic, and her expectations of what it will be like are not what she finds. Her sanctuary is flawed. Storms are often a symbol of impending troubles, so you can have great storm clouds rolling in from the west, covering the sun.

POINT OF VIEW:

You should use third person, past tense, an objective attitude and limited omniscient knowledge. The narrator position follows the girl until the sheriff comes, then it follows him.

Watch the objective attitude of the narrative voice. You will not be able to say, "It was a nice day." You will have to tell your readers what the day was like, but you will not be able to make any value judgments. You can call the city streets "dirty" but not say it was a shame that they were that way. You can have the character care, but with an objective attitude, the narrative voice cannot care one way or the other what happens.

WAYS TO GET IN AND OUT OF THE CHARACTER'S MIND:

It is an accepted practice in writing fiction that the more sophisticated the reader the more subtle can be the writing and the less help the reader needs to understand what's going on. This narrative is to be written for sophisticated adult readers. You can do almost anything you want when you're showing the young woman thinking. If your readers were to be young or untrained, you'd have to be careful to give lots of directions for reading so as to avoid confusion about whether you were giving the character's exact thoughts or letting your readers know the kinds of things she's thinking.

This is the difference:

She thought about how good it would be to be home.

In this passage the reader is told the kinds of things she thought about but not her thoughts.

If you want your reader to see her thoughts (be in her mind) then it could be said like this:

She thought, It sure will be good to be home.

When you're going into her mind to let the readers know what she's thinking, you may use one of the following techniques:

1.	Quote marks:

She looked up at the tall buildings on both sides of her. "They trap me here. It's like they don't want me to leave." or, her thoughts can be labeled as thoughts: She thought, as she looked up at the tall buildings on both sides of her, "They trap me here. It's like they don 't. . . . "

2.	Italicize (if hand written or if typed, you should use underlining): Underlining indicates to your publisher that these passages are to be in italics.

She looked up at the tall buildings on both sides of her. <u>They trap me here. It's like they don't want me to leave.</u>

3.	Use the narrative voice to tell about the thoughts she has:

She looked up at the tall buildings on both sides of her and thought they looked like they didn't want her to leave.

4.	Not label the thoughts at all:

She looked up at the tall buildings on both sides of her. They trap me here. It's like they don't want me to leave.

The shift of person and tense will be all a good reader will need to recognize that the thoughts are coming from the character's mind.

In dialogues she has in her mind, it should not be necessary to use quote marks:

When she stepped into the kitchen, she could smell again her grandmother's fresh bread baking. I must have been about nine or ten the last time I smelled that. She ran her hand over the cold and dusty wood-burning stove. She heard her own long-ago, little-girl voice:
Is that cookies, Grandma?
No, Jane. Bread.
Can I have some now?
When it's done—about five more minutes.
With real butter?
Of course you can, dear. Let me get you a glass of milk.

You should draw a rough map of the property and a floor plan of the main part of the house. If you don't do this you might not have a clear picture of the action, and your readers won't "see" the place and action. More about this in a moment.

47

As you write your story, remember that the point of this exercise is to create moods in your readers.

This is a fairly complicated set of instructions, much more so than you probably need (or maybe even should have) but it represents the type of thinking that a well-planned story might require. There's a feeling in some people that pre-writing thinking stifles imagination, and this might be true for an experienced writer.

At some level, even a very good writer must make these decisions, even though they may not be made on the conscious level. You probably won't need to go into such detail on your next story attempt.

Notes like the following might be helpful.

1. Nature of the girl's problem _____

    _____

2. Description of the beast if real _____

    _____

    _____

3. If the beast is not real but in her mind, why is it there and what does it represent?

    A. Why _____

    _____

    B. What _____

    _____

4. The objects and conditions used to create the three moods
    Mood 1) _____

    _____

    Mood 2) _____

Mood 3) _____

_____

5. The symbols planned for each scene
   A. In the city
      1. Her apartment _____

      2. City streets _____
   B. Highway out of town
      1. On the road with her _____

      2. Alongside the road _____
   C. Country roads
      1. The view _____

      2. The weather _____

   D. First view of the old house _____

   E. First day feelings of security _____

   F. Terror of the first night's experience with her fears _____

11

Satire

Satire is a special kind of criticism. It's a form of writing which allows readers to laugh at themselves or the situations they find themselves in and not take offense and automatically reject the criticism.

This is a difficult thing for a writer to do, and one of the hardest aspects of this kind of writing is to avoid being sarcastic, which likely will happen with beginning writers. It's easy to slip into sarcasm. Although sarcasm is a part of satire, you will have to be careful how you use it. Because of the nature of this type of criticism, there will be sarcasm in your writing if you are satiric even if you don't plan to have it there.

Sarcasm in satire is inherent in the exaggeration of the situation or process being criticized. There's no way to totally avoid it. Blatant sarcasm, as in this reference to, for instance, the city council: "Our wonderful new city council, in its infinite wisdom. . ." will detract from the effectiveness of your writing.

There are some other aspects of this type of writing which you'll want to keep in mind:
1. The object, situation, or process that the writer is criticizing must be clearly identified for the reader. The reader must know what the point of the attack is, but the writing will be more effective if this is not stated boldly.

2. To avoid offense and allow the reader to enjoy the satire, there should be a distance built between the reader and the situation. This is why, in many satires, the characters are animals like rabbits and penguins, little people, giants, characters from other planets or inanimate objects given life for the purposes of the satire.

   Sometimes characters like Gulliver and Alice travel to strange lands or impossible places. In some works, there is a distortion of time, or the characters are put on a distant island or even another planet, as they are in some of the works of William Golding and Kurt Vonnegut Jr. This makes it easy for the reader to laugh at the characters and their predicaments, taking some of the "sting" out of the criticism.

3. In most satire there is a degree of innocence shown by the main character. This gives the writer the opportunity to have someone ask questions, the answering of which allows the writer to make the points desired.

4. Exaggeration is an essential ingredient. Satirists wish to criticize situations, so they analyze what caused the situations in the first place, then, in their fictitious situations, they exaggerate both the causes and the conditions they produce.

5. There is irony in some well written satire. This is very difficult to produce, but it would be good for you if you were to try to create it. You might start with looking up irony in a dictionary of literary terms, and then, when you have the situation for your satire worked out, you should plan on trying to make some aspect of it ironic.

In this exercise, you are to satirize a situation in your life. There must be dozens of things you'd like to criticize about yourself or your situation. Below are some examples of things I'd find easy to satirize in my life. For instance, I was a public school teacher for 30 years, and in our school system we teach the children to tell time in the first grade. Every room in the high school where I taught has a clock. There are clocks in all the halls. Every teacher has a watch, and at least half of the kids have watches. We ring bells to tell the kids when classes end.

If I were to write a satire about this condition, I'd create a situation where there'd be a public health inspector who would come to a high school to examine the building and the situation because of a report of rats. This person would be the innocent traveler in the school—able to ask lots of questions.

The inspector would find that the rats are a result of piles of uneaten lunch food found behind the school. It would turn out in my satire that none of the kids are able to eat lunch because the bell system has broken. The kids have learned to be hungry for lunch at the ringing of the lunch bell, and since it has not worked, none of them have been able to eat lunch.

I might also talk about our very expensive football stadium. Its cost is justified by us saying it was built for the education of the children. "It is important for the students to have a nice stadium for their home games." But the fifty yard line seats are reserved for the paying adults and the kids are made to sit near the end zones.

As you can see, in my life there are situations that would be easy to criticize with satire. It will help if you read a number of satiric pieces by Art Buchwald. He's a clever political and social satirist. If you were to make an outline of a number of his writings, you'd see a pattern emerge that you could follow.

Usually he:
1. Introduces his subject by a bit of background (history)
2. Sets up a situation where he's able to have his narrative voice ask questions, and creates a distance between the reader and the situation by a distortion of time, characters and/or place
3. Has the rest of most of his pieces consist of dialogues between his "investigator" and some official
4. Ends about half of his pieces with a bit of ironic observation

One of the problems that beginning writers have with humor is that when they try to be funny they almost always end up being corny. Try not to be funny. Humor is an essential part of satire, but the "fun" in satire is in the reader recognizing the situation and how ridiculous it is and not in what the narrative voice says.

After you have picked the part of your life you'd like to criticize, you should invent some reason for your narrative voice to be investigating this situation, or some reason for the voice to be visiting you. You could have your voice be a distant cousin, a new friend or a newspaper reporter.

You then, in your mind, should exaggerate the situation to get a picture of how to write the piece. The exaggeration can be as great as you want it to be.

You will have to put that "distance" between the reader of your piece and the created situation. You can do this by placing your story in the future, making up obviously phony names for the people involved, placing the action on a place other than Earth or, if on Earth, in a made-up-place (such as Alice or Gulliver found themselves), or you could make the characters non-people such as those in *The Hobbit* or *Watership Down* or the comic strip characters like Mickey Mouse or that possum in the swamp in *Pogo* who said "We have met the enemy and they is us."

The innocent character, when he/she is introduced to your exaggerated situation, can ask questions which will give you the opportunity to demonstrate the difference between what would be rational to do and what is now being done in your life that you want to criticize.

12

Using Tenses

Consistency of tense use by the narrative voice in fiction is considered the normal convention. This means that when an author starts a story in past tense, the reader expects to continue reading in past tense until the story ends.

Of course, there are conditions within a narrative voice's use of tense when the tense must shift, but, in conventional prose, there have always been logical justifications for the shifts. Examples of some of these conditions might help:

1. When the narrative voice is created as limited omniscient—can get into the minds of the characters—then those thoughts of the characters can be in any tense and even shift from one tense to another. This is not necessarily a case of the narrative voice talking to a reader, but rather, the narrative voice showing the reader what a character's thinking, and people/characters think in all tenses and shift often. Notice the tense selection in the following example:

    John walked into the room and thought, "Boy, am I late."

    In this case, the narrative voice is speaking to the reader in **past tense** but puts the reader into the mind of the character who is thinking in **present tense**.

    Characters can and do think in all of the tenses, and this does not affect the narrative voice tense at all. Notice the shifts here:

    He glanced over to the far corner of the room where Janet was sitting with the new senior boy and thought, "If she looks up and sees that I'm just getting here, she'll know how late I am. I've got to cross the room and look like I've been here a long time. Once I'm relaxed in conversation, then I'll be okay." He joined a small group of jocks standing by the kitchen door talking about football. When he had filled his mouth with crackers, he glanced up and caught Janet's eye. He saluted her with a cracker and smiled and thought, "I got here at least half an hour ago and have been watching you talk with that guy the whole time. That's right, go on the offensive—best defense." He moved toward her.

    The narrative voice speaks to the reader in past tense in this passage, but notice the tense

53

shifting the character goes through: *Boy, am I late.* **present** . . *she'll know how late I am.* **future** I *got here. . . past. This is* a normal way for people to shift tenses when they think, but in this passage, the narrative voice is consistent in its tense use.

2. When the narrative voice takes the reader on a journey into the past or the future, there's not really a shift in the tense of the narrative voice. The main tense is still the same, and the shifts are justified. Notice the shifts here:

> *When his horse started limping, Jake knew he would soon no longer be able to ride and he might be too late. Even now he stood a slim chance of getting to the fort on time. He has no way of knowing this, but he will be too late to warn the colonel of the attack. The buildings will be burning when he gets there, and the bodies will have been scalped. The women and children will be gone. Kidnaped, taken as slaves.*
>
> *He rode as long as he could, then walked beside his horse over the endless, slow-rolling hills. He should have listened to Bill when he had told him to take both horses. He hadn't been able to imagine country like this. Nor had it seemed possible his horse could pull up lame.*
>
> *As he came to the crest of each hill, he got on his horse and stood in the saddle to see as far into his future as he could. As yet, there were no buildings, but there was a dark smudge on the horizon. Like a line of black clouds. . .or smoke.*

The narrative voice starts with past: . . .*horse started limping* then shifts to **future:** . . .*he will be too late to warn the colonel of the attack. The buildings will be burning.* . .then back to **past:** *He rode as long as he could.* . . now **past-perfect:** *He had not been able to imagine country like this. It hadn't seemed possible his horse could pull up lame.* **and ends with past**: *As yet, there were no buildings, but there was a dark . . .*

The following exercise is designed to show you how you can use tenses in a creative way. It's necessary for you to read some examples of unusual tense use. J.P. Donlevy and Richard Brautigan are two men who *play* successfully with tenses to develop theme. When first encountered this can be disconcerting, but with a little reader effort, it can become an enlightening experience. A shifting of tenses has the effect of distorting the normal time flow without the necessity of informing the reader (outside of the story line) that this is being done. Employed by an artist, this can become an effective stylistic technique.

Your library should have this short book. In the first four pages of Brautigan's *So The Wind Won't Blow It All Away*, you'll find examples of this intentional distortion of normal time frames. The distortion is designed to create and recreate the past as an integral part of the character's living present. Initially, this is confusing, but it does give a certain charm to the narrative, and helps the reader understand what Brautigan is trying to make clear in his art. He forces an immediacy to his childhood experiences.

He creates for his reader a period in his life, from vignettes from his past, which he combines into a novella. As we all do when examining our pasts, he makes himself the central character, and, ignoring the more conventional conceptions of time flow, moves himself back and forth in time, with his main concern being the feelings created. We accept this because of our understanding of the nature of memory—that the scenes of our past are not locked into logical sequence but may flash at random into our consciousness.

To understand his use of tenses in his work, it's important that you examine his story with care.

To help you keep this straight, you should justify Brautigan's tense shifting, taking excerpts from the text to use as examples. You may not be right in your decisions about why he shifts as he does, but that's not important. The point of the exercise is to have you make logical justification for the shifts. It's important only that the shifts work for you. There must be some reason given for:

A. The tense he uses to start the narrative

B. Each of the subsequent shifts, both to new non-past tenses and shifts back to the original tense

It would then help you control your tenses if you were to write a narrative in which you were to intentionally distort the conventions of tense use. In the narration, you could label each shift (indicating what tense you're shifting into and the reason for the shifting), so that when you go back over it, you'll understand what you were trying to do.

Below are some examples of justifications that have been made for Brautigan's piece. This does not mean that they're what the author had in mind or that they should satisfy you. You'll have to invent your own justifications for why he shifts tenses.

1. The end of paragraph three from page one of *So The Wind Won't Blow It All Away*

> *They had very good hamburgers but I wasn't hungry. For the rest of my life I'll think (1) about that hamburger. . .down my cheeks. The waitress will be looking away because she doesn't (2) like to. . .embarrass me. I'm (3) the only customer in the restaurant.*

  1. Future tense. He shifts from the past tense, the main narrative tense used, to future tense. He imagines what will happen because of a decision he made in the past.

  2. He shifts from the future tense, the place his imagination has taken him, to present tense. This means he's using the present tense for his narration of what will happen in the future so as to take the reader with him in his imaginary travels into his own future. The present tense here makes the reader see the waitress as he sees her see him in his mind's future.

55

3. Present tense. The interest in the shift here is not just in tense but in the significance of the tense use. He already has the reader in the present tense, but it is the present he has created in the future. He now dissolves the idea of the future mode and puts the reader with him in the present, continuing to use the present tense. He's done this so that the reader can experience the event along with him, even though he's creating it in his mind as he sees it happening in the future.

2. This gets confusing here, because, when he takes the reader into his past, and then makes the past live by treating it like it's the present, he (in the past) thinks about what it will be like in the future. But, he already knows what the future will hold, because he has lived it, for we started with him at this future time, which really is the present. Brautigan goes through all of these changes so that the reader can live in his (Brautigan's) mind's experiences with what we call *me*. When we think about ourselves, we understand that what we see ourselves as is a composite of the many people we have been in the past and not just the persons we are now. The *me* that each of us knows is made up of many *me's* and we each have not just the present one that other people we have just met know. They're not aware that each of us has a *me* that is made up of the *me* when we were ten years old, and one that was *me* when we were thirteen and so on. All of the memories each of us have of ourselves make up what we understand we are.

In order for this author to give this understanding to his reader, he has to create a distortion of an ordinary acceptance of how time works. In most books, the character who is shown to the reader is the only one the reader knows. All the other characters who have gone into making up that one character have faded into the past and have died there. Brautigan brings some of the dead Brautigans to life by his tense shifting.

13

Speaking Patterns

One of the more difficult skills you must have is writing dialogue so that it reads as if real people were talking together. Beginning writers have a tendency to have all of their characters sound alike. Like teenagers or English teachers.

Each of the characters you create will have a unique background which should dictate how that character will speak. The educations, intelligence, family backgrounds, attitudes toward themselves their families and society, and the parts of the country they come from all influence what people sound like.

When you create a character, these conditions have to be taken into account. You must consider each of the contributing factors of a character's background when deciding how that character would speak about events and to and about people.

It'd be good practice for you to create situations where people of diverse backgrounds speak together. By mixing them you can more effectively differentiate their speaking modes.

The following examples will give you an idea of what I mean by this suggestion.

Boy With a Ball Scenario

A small boy, Billy, lives in a high rise apartment with his out-of-work mother. He asks her if he can go out and play with his ball while she does the dishes. While he is playing with it, the ball rolls down the hill and into traffic. Chasing the ball, Billy runs into the street and is lightly brushed by a passing car, which causes all traffic to stop.

A neighbor sees this happen and is also able to hear Billy's mother call out to him from her third floor window.

Billy's mother runs down the stairs but falls in the lobby and breaks her arm. The police are called on a CB radio, and, when they arrive, they escort Billy to his apartment building and find his mother in the lobby.

The neighbor has called an ambulance for the mother, which takes her and her son to the hospital emergency room. A social worker is called by the doctor because Billy was injured while not being watched by his mother. The policeman who investigates the accident tells his wife about it, and the next day she has a phone conversation with her friend about it.

The social worker interviews the mother to find out if there was child neglect. There is a police report of the accident and this all gets in the paper.

As you can see, there is a great deal of opportunity here for many different "voices." There are Billy, his mother, the neighbor lady, the policeman, the policeman's wife and her friend, the ambulance drivers, the doctor, the nurses, the social worker, the newspaper reporter and an objective narrative voice.

It doesn't matter how you set up this kind of an exercise as long as you're practicing creating speech patterns. You can present the speakers as voices talking to the reader or to each other. This can be in one long narrative, or it can be in small segments.

Examples of some of these voices:

Objective Narrator

It was in about the middle of July when Billy was hit by the car and his mother broke her arm running down the stairs trying to catch him before he could run in the road. She didn't know, when she looked out of the window on tile third floor and saw him running toward the road, that when trying to help him she would fall and would have to be taken to the hospital along with her son. . .

Neighbor

I was sittin' in that old chair I keep facing out toward the highway, and Billy was bouncing his ball agin' the wall like he likes to. Such a nice little kid. I don't unnerstan' why she don't watch him closer. I had one, I sure would. Anyway, I was just sittin' there. I do that a lot since I lost my Harry. I guess I was about half asleep, and l heard this yell from in the lobby, and right away I heard the screech of brakes, and I didn't know where to look.

Mother

I was just doing the dishes, I like to keep a clean house. I think that's important to do that—keep a clean house I mean, not just to do the lunch dishes, I always do the dishes just after we eat, I mean keeping the house nice for both of us. A person never knows when somebody will drop in—not that we get so much company and all, it's just what I like to do. Good for Billy. I think it's a good example to set, to keep things clean and neat. Anyway, there I was at the sink and I could look out the window and see the road, and the first thing I know, I could see Billy running down the hill toward the road, so. . .

58

Boy

I was playin' bouncy ball and it hit a rock—the rock made it go down the hill. I didn't throw it down, it just went there. I see it go to the road and I remember my mom say not to go in the road, but I don't want my ball to get hurt so I run and see if I can catch up with it before it goes into the road 'cuz I know I can't go in the road, my mom already told me that, so I run and try an catch it, but it sees me and goes faster. I think it'll get clear to town 'fore I catch it but. . .

You might even put your characters together like this:

Social Worker and Mother

Mother: What ya want?

Social Worker: I'm from the social services office. My name is Mrs. Phillips. May I come in and talk to you for a few moments?

Mother: Sure, I guess there's no harm in that. Sit down. Now, what do you want?

Social Worker: My office sent me here because of a report the police department sent to our child abuse department.

Mother: Now, just hold on there. Billy's not been abused by nobody. Anybody says he has been is lyin'. Now, I think you better just go right back and tell them at your "office" that—

Social Worker: Mrs. Brown, we have been asked to talk to you about what happened on the thirteenth of this month when Billy got hit by the car. It is not our intention to cause you any trouble, but it is important that we get all the information we can, because in a case where a child is hurt, and was unattended at the time, there is always a question of neglect.

Mother: Are you here to try to say I did wrong or something? I'll tell you right now, I do a good job with Billy. I don't have much money to buy clothes like you got on, but I do what I can.

Social Worker: No, Mrs. Brown, we are not trying to place blame on anyone. We are just looking into the circumstances of the accident.

59

> Mother: *That better be all, cause you come in here with your big words and your fancy clothes talkin' about takin' my boy away from me.*

Policeman's Wife and Friend on Phone

Marsha: *Hello.*

Joan: *Hello, Marsha, is that you?*

Marsha: *Oh, Joan! How you doing? How's Jack? Is he feeling better?*

Joan: *Everything's about the same on this end. The doctor said Jack may have a small ulcer, but he'll be okay.*

Marsha: *No wonder he has an ulcer, the hours he puts in. It's a miracle he hasn't had a heart attack, you know. He gonna retire?*

Joan: *Retire. He's only forty-eight and the work usually isn't too tough. Just yesterday, the biggest call he had was when some kid on the south side got hit by a car.*

Marsha: *That's terrible, what happened? Did Jack tell you?*

Joan: *Sure he did. I guess the kid just wasn't watching, and he was hit. Well, actually, just bruised. But, Jack said the kid's mother wasn't even watching. Just let him play out in the road.*

Marsha: *That's disgusting.*

Joan: *Oh, that's not the half of it. When the mother saw what happened, she took off down the stairs of the apartment building to get to her boy and she fell down the stairs. Nearly killed herself; she did. I think she broke a few bones.*

Marsha: *That's some weird story. Just think, not only did the boy get hurt from her negligence, so did she. I guess that mother got what she deserved, anyway.*

Joan: *Well, I don't know about that, but Jack said he did call social services, and they'll take care of it.*

Marsha: *Oh no. My roast, it's burning. I got ta go, I'll see you later.*

Joan: *Yea, bye-bye.*

You should be aware that there has been no attempt to make these model dialogues realistic, but just to show you how background and characteristics influence the way characters talk. There are no descriptions of bodies in the models, just voices. This would make pretty tiring reading. You must avoid having what are called disembodied voices talking to each other.

It might be a good exercise for you to take the dialogues in these models conversations and put bodies on the speakers then show how the characters use their bodies to help them exchange ideas. The way characters use their bodies is also governed by their experiences. Authors spend much time "watching" how people move. This would be a good exercise for you, studying how people use their bodies to help them get their ideas across to other people.

60

14

Information Given Indirectly
Through Description

Much of the information that readers gain from both fiction and non-fiction is in the form of feelings and attitudes they acquire because of the ways the authors describe situations and objects. Authors are like gods in their creative processes. They have the whole universe to choose from and can create and ignore any part of it at their will.

Those things they choose to ignore will not exist in the minds of their readers, and those they describe will exist for their readers in the forms they choose. If a writer wants a reader to see, from the side window of a speeding automobile, a dog on a hillside, he/she can create it, and in the reader's mind there will be a dog on a hillside. Conversely, if he/she doesn't want a dog to be there, the writer won't mention it, and there will be no dog.

If the writer wants to give the reader the information only that there is a dog on a hillside, once the dog has been created, the job is done, but much of the value in the transmission of information is in non-specific information the writer can relay to his reader by the detail and subject of the description used.

For a number of reasons, an author might feel it would be more effective to convey information in subtle ways rather than to be specific. Suppose the writer wants to give the reader the feeling (information) that there is something the dog is guarding and that there might be something sinister or dangerous about the situation.

The reader could be given clues to the information that, without the reader being aware of it, would relay what the writer wants the reader to feel (know). The following two examples demonstrate this process.

Example #1

Through the window on the right side of the car, the man could see, standing on a slight hill just off the edge of the road, a large dog. When he got near enough to see details clearly, he could see the dog was wagging its tail and looking toward his car. The dog remained in the same spot but was almost prancing. It would first lift its left foot and then its right. When the car drew quite near, the tail slowed its movement and then stopped and hung

61

down, but the dog continued to watch the car. The man turned and looked back just before he turned the corner and saw the dog still watching him.

In this paragraph you understand that the dog is lost and is looking for its master. You know this because of the way the behavior of the dog is described.

Example #2

The man could see, from the right side of the car, the sun dropping over the crest of the hill. He could just make out the shape of a large dog standing near the crest. The sun was still too bright for the image to be seen clearly, but he had the feeling the animal was staring at him. When the car had gone a bit further, he could make out some detail and could see the rigid stance and the lowered head which turned with the car's passage. Just after he entered the curve, the man turned back and looked at the dog again. Now the sun was reflected in the dog's eyes, making them glow. His last impression was of the two shining eyes following him around the bend.

In this example you know that the dog is guarding something. You have a feeling of some evil in the situation because of the light in the dog's eyes. The setting sun behind the dog, making the animal hard to see, suggests that the dog may be hiding something or that there is something that you are not meant to see.

Some of the information (feeling) transmitted by these two passages is conveyed by the use of symbols, some by the use of non-symbolic images familiar to most readers, and some by suggestion. Almost the only specific information given about the dog in both instances is that the dog is standing on a hill watching the car, yet when you read the two passages you have very different feelings (information) about why the dog is there. This technique is very common in fiction and is also used effectively in advertisements, political speeches, newspaper commentaries and magazine articles.

In this exercise you'll describe a scene four times. In each one you'll give different information to your reader by:
1. What details you describe
2. The ways you position the people, events and objects
3. The symbols you choose to use
4. The dialogue you choose to let the reader hear
5. The emphasis you place on actions, events and relationships

You're to describe a sunset as seen by one or two people standing on the edge of the Grand Canyon. You're to use third person, past tense for the first three pieces and a non-involved, non-present, limited omniscient narrative voice for the last one.

FIRST SCENE:

A newlywed couple is watching the sunset at the Grand Canyon and this is the first night of their honeymoon. They both, in different ways, are anxious for the sun to set. She sees the setting of the sun as a loss of her childhood and her known security. He sees the setting of the sun as the beginning of their life together and is anxious for it to set. This information in this paragraph must be given to your reader in non-direct ways. You're not to have the characters think these things or have this information brought out directly in dialogue or have the narrative voice tell the reader.

SECOND SCENE:

A man and woman are married and one of them (you have a choice of which one) is terminally ill. They're looking at the same scene. This is to be their last trip together. In fact, this may be their last sunset seen together. They're much in love. But, the reader must feel (know) the sadness and the finality of the last sunset. The reader must not be told directly but must understand that one of these people is dying and must appreciate the pain the other one is feeling.

THIRD SCENE:

A woman and her seven-year-old child are watching the same scene. The divorce has finally come through, and she and her son are on their way back to her parents' home to live. Their old life is over. The family is split. These two are together, but alone.

FOURTH SCENE:

A young woman on her way west to start a new job and a new life has stopped to watch the sun set. The world is opening up for her. She has left the confines of the city and the restrictions imposed upon her by her family and their conservative ways. She's excited but frightened by the wonder and the uncertain nature of her new life.

15

Controlling Structure

It's easy in conversation to recognize that the way things are said is as important to meaning as are the words used to say them. This is just as true in writing, but it's not so obvious nor is it as easy to do. In this exercise you'll practice controlling your reader's reactions to what you're saying by the careful selection of your words and the ways you put them together.

This is a skill Hemingway became famous for, but most authors have it to a greater or lesser degree. Ken Kesey, starts his *Sometimes a Great Notion* clearly in command of this skill. There may/ be so much effort here to use structure to compliment content that it overshadows the other important aspects of what he's doing, but it will serve as a good example for you to study. Kesey opens his book with a description of a river which functions as a metaphor for the powerful flow of family ties through three generations of loggers in Oregon.

1.
Along the western slopes of the Oregon Coastal Range. . .come look: the hysterical crashing of tributaries as they merge into the Wakonda Auga River.. .
2.
The first little washes flashing like thick rushing winds through sheep sorrel and clover, ghost fern and nettle, sheering, cutting. . .forming branches. (3) Then, through bearberry and salmonberry, blueberry and blackberry, the branches crashing into creeks, into streams. (4) Finally, in the foothills, through tamarack and sugar pine, shittim bark and silver spruce—and the green and blue mosaic of douglas fir—the actual river falls five hundred feet. . .and look: opens out upon the fields.

In just two short paragraphs, only four sentences, Kesey gives us a great deal. He presents us with some factual material, but more importantly, he transmits a feeling for the scene by his sentence structuring and his careful word choices.

In the **first sentence** he introduces us to a long-range view of the entire watershed area and directs our eyes to the western side of the mountains. He uses ellipsis (. . .) to indicate there is more. He tells us to come closer for a look at one particular river. He ends the first sentence with ellipsis again, indicating that there is more to be seen. This first sentence is a fragment, not complete. The view he wants us to have is not complete either. A nice way to tell us this.

64

The **second sentence** is also a fragment. We're not done yet. By starting his sentence with *The first* we are told we are being given an introduction to the start of the river-forming process. Here is step one and an introduction to step two. He must want us to hear the sounds of the beginnings of the river as we read. In mountains, the melting snow and the rains form little fingers of water that form his "washes." Notice his concentration on words that have sounds similar to what we'd hear if we were standing near running water. There are a great many high-pitched sounds. Read the second sentence aloud and listen to the *st, th,* and *s,* sounds. Just like tiny fingers of water rushing through leaves and twigs.

In the **third sentence**, presenting us with continuity by the use of *then*, we're told to look at larger branches (We were introduced to the idea in the last of the second sentence). These branches would burble and bubble over rocks and logs. Notice the many words that have *b* and *k* sounds. There still are the *s* and *sh* sounds, but now the water is moving faster and makes a heavier sound. Still a fragment. We haven't seen it all yet.

The **fourth sentence** starts with *Finally* letting us know that we're going to be presented with the whole picture at last. And we have the first complete sentence of the book. He imposes an interesting rhythm on this sentence. We have the feeling that we have been running down the side of the mountain with the water. Faster and faster through the trees—and then we break out of the cover and can see the river as it broadens out, slows down and flows away. To produce this feeling, he rushes us with words describing the trees—they come quickly, one after another, then he stops us with the ellipsis, which tells us there is more. He commands us to look. Again he stops us, this time with a full colon: we're out of breath and need the rest. Then he presents us with the view we have been waiting for—the whole river.

It's very obvious in these two paragraphs that he's manipulating us. We feel used when we read it. Even so, this kind of writing is hard to do and do well. You'll have a chance to do it in this exercise. This will be a very structured experience for you, and it will not leave you much room in which to maneuver. It will not be a very creative exercise, but it will give you experience in controlling your reader's reactions to what you write.

You're to write a third person, past tense, non-involved, limited omniscient, objective account. (Wow! You may want to go back and look again at those choices) of a young man stuck on a secondary road in Iowa. He has spent the night sleeping along the side of the road. There are very few cars or trucks which use this stretch of highway. The man is intelligent and very bored with being in the corn belt of America. A truck comes along but doesn't stop for him.

You are to write **three paragraphs**.

The first one will start with the young man rising and walking to the roadway. He'll see the reflection of the sun off a windshield in the distance and think of the advantages and the disadvantages of it being a car or a truck. The first paragraph will end as the truck gets to him.

The second paragraph will begin when the truck starts to pass him and will end when the truck is just past him.

The third paragraph will begin just as soon as the truck is past him and will end when the truck is out of sight.

PARAGRAPH # 1

First Sentence:

You'll want your reader to feel as bored as the young man who is thinking that he'll never get out of this section of Iowa. This sentence should be at least 150 words long. The man should be doing something that is inconsequential, but he should be doing it with great concentration. Your readers should be frustrated with the sentence and reading of the activity and have the feeling they'll never get out of the passage, much like the man feels he'll never get out of Iowa.

Second Sentence:

When the man sees a speck of light reflected off a windshield, he wonders if it's from a car or a truck. This sentence should be a compound-complex one of about 100 words. In the first half of the sentence, he should think of the advantages and disadvantages of the light being reflected from a car, and in the second half, he should think of the advantages and disadvantages of the light being reflected from a truck.

This diagram of the second sentence might be helpful:

Jack saw, far off down the roadway, a speck of light and wondered if it might be a car or a truck which might pick him up and. . .

        advantages
thought of the   +   *of it being a car;*
        disadvantages

(Here you will need a conjunction such as): but...and...however...and a comma (,)

(And now the second half of the compound sentence)

        advantages
he also thought of the + *of it being a truck.*
        disadvantages

I know this looks complicated, but it's not hard to understand if you think of it this way: The reader needs to feel the same way the young man feels about the approaching vehicle. He wonders if it is a car or a truck and thinks of the good and bad aspects of both. This is done in a compound sentence so that the reader can feel the young man weighing the problem in his mind. The tenses can get tricky in this sentence. Your narrative voice speaks in past tense, *The young man was standing on the side of the road,* but when he sees the speck of light and wonders what it might be reflected from, you must first shift into present tense for his thoughts and then into future perfect: . . .He thought, *If that's a car then it might be driven by a nice salesman who (now the shift) might stop and it'd be great if he'd have. . .*

Third Sentence:

This sentence will have the man recognize the outline of a truck and try to figure out where he'd hear the air brakes if the truck were to stop for him. Pick some place a good distance down the road for this. This sentence should be about 60-80 words long.

The rest of the first paragraph should contain sentences of gradually decreasing length until it ends with a one-word sentence. This progressive shortening of the length of the sentences will give the reader the feeling that the closer the truck gets to the man the faster, it seems to be approaching. The fourth sentence should be about 50 words long, the fifth about 30, the sixth about 15, the seventh about ten, the eighth about five and the ninth should be one.

During this period of waiting, you can have the man thinking, getting his things together or straightening his clothing and hair. The reader should be feeling anxiety and hope as the truck gets closer.

PARAGRAPH # 2

The second paragraph will be one sentence long and should take as long to read as it takes a 50 foot truck traveling 55 miles an hour to pass the point where the man is standing. To give the reader the feeling of confusion at this explosion of sensory input, the sentence should contain no abstractions and should be made up of fragments and not be a complete sentence—it should not have a subject.

The sensory impressions should be mixed so that two and three word, word-groups, describe the scene. Sight and sound could be described in the first group at the same time, and the next group could combine sound and feeling and so on. The two and three word word-groups can be separated by commas, ellipsis or dashes. They should look like this: *Towering silver roar. . .dusty wind suck. . .* and so on for ten or twelve more words. The second paragraph will end as soon as the truck speeds past the man. This should give your reader the same feelings the man experiences. There should be a confusion of images and sensations. During times of great and rapid sensory input, we don't have time to think about anything. We have time only to receive the sensory information. This is what the man feels and your reader should also.

PARAGRAPH #3

The structuring of the third paragraph will be a reversal of the first. It will start with a one-word sentence, then have a longer one, possibly five words. The third might have twelve or fifteen words and so on until the paragraph ends with a long sentence just like first paragraph starts. This should give the reader the feeling that the further the truck is from the man the slower it recedes from him. The young man should end up doing, in the last part of the third paragraph, the same kind of concentrated activity he's doing in the first part of the first paragraph. It would be best if he were not doing the exact same thing, but an activity close enough to the same thing so that the reader gets the feeling that nothing has happened. This would be the same feeling that the man might have—nothing is going on at that spot in Iowa.

To further increase the reader's feeling of being on the side of the road with the man, you could employ your understanding of the Doppler effect. This is the phenomenon that when an object approaches, its' sound has a higher pitch than it does when it's moving away. Think back to when you watched an Indianapolis 500 race. When the cars approach the camera/microphone they seem to scream, and when they're in front of the camera the sound drops in pitch, and, as they go away, the scream changes to a low-pitched roar.

This same sound effect would be heard by the man on the side of the road as the truck roars past him. This Doppler effect can be created by the sounds of the words you chose to use.

In the last part of the first paragraph, the last 40 or 50 words, you should use as many plosives, sibilants and fricatives as you can. These are high-pitched sounds. They're used in letters like s, *th, e, i, f; to k ch, t, b* and *p*. Use words like *scream, soar, seem, this, fast,* and *pitch.*

In the first part of the third paragraph, the first 40 or 50 words, you should use as many words that have low sounds as you can. These have letters like w, *r, m, a, o, and l . You* should use words like *rumble, move, go, rubber, low, wheel* and *wobble.*

On the next page is a graphic representation of the structuring of these three paragraphs. Of course, your paper will not look like an hour glass. The numbers correspond to the number of words in each sentence. As you get closer to the one-word sentence you should count syllables.

150-   Rises and performs meaningless activity
  110-   Compound-complex sentence: Sees light reflection
    85-   Estimates when he will hear air brakes
      60
       47
        35

Paragraph # 1   23-   High Pitched Sounds
         15
          9
           6
            3
             1 word

Paragraph #   2 Sentence fragment made up of two and three word word-groups which
          are concrete descriptions of the man's sensory impression

            1 word
           3
         9
        15

Paragraph # 3   23-   Low Pitched Sounds
       35
     47
    60
   85
  100-   Resumption of Meaningless Activity

16

Creating Characters

Probably the most important element in fiction is the establishment and development of characters. If your reader is not intensely interested in your main characters and what happens to them, you have little chance of holding any interest in your story.

A good practice exercise for you as you learn to write is to create character sketches. These are fairly short, 800 to 1,000 words long, that give your reader a feeling for your "people".

You'll have to have access to a library for the first part of this exercise where you'll find examples of writers who show their readers their characters' physical appearance in ways that have become clichés. This means you're looking for examples of ways not to write. These will be easiest to find, therefore, in less than great literature. Try young adult, romance, or historical romance novels first.

You should find examples of descriptions of physical appearance using methods similar to the following:
1. A character looks in the mirror and the narrative voice or the character describes what is seen.
2. Another person looks at the character and the narrative voice tells the reader what is seen.
3. The narrative voice tells the reader what the character looks like in an abstracted section—it has nothing to do with the story line.

This will give you examples of what not to do in giving your reader the physical characteristics of your characters. You should now find more sophisticated physical description techniques. Again, library work will be necessary.

You should find two or three examples of authors giving their readers physical descriptions in which the authors let the readers discover the appearance of the characters by seeing the characters in action so that the descriptions appear to be a natural part of the story line.

This will give you examples of what to do in creating the physical descriptions of your characters.

To practice this, you should write just those passages in which your description would occur in the beginning of a piece of short fiction. The passages below will show you what I mean.

Paragraph 1:

John, the tallest boy who had ever gone to Woodward, could never be on time for math class. It was one. . .

Paragraph 2:

. . .he even had to stoop to come into the door. This never seemed to bother him, because, after ducking his head onto his thin chest, he always looked up smiling.

Paragraph 4:

I opened my book to the page and pushed it across to John. He placed one long finger on the answer and looked up with those strangely violet eyes—and smiled at me!

This gives you an example of how your physical description can be integrated into the actions of the character and not have the description seem out of place and a contrivance of the author.

Next, you should find an example of how a good author creates a character. This can be done in two parts:
1. The actions of the character
2. The motives of the character

In the actions list you should list and give examples for:
1. How the character moves (body actions)
2. What the character owns
3. How the character talks
   A. Vocabulary
   B. Sentence length and variety
   C. Common expressions
   D. Style (formal/informal)
   E. How the character deals with people when talking with them.
   F. How the character uses body action to help him communicate ideas
4. What the character likes to do
5. How the character treats objects
6. What the character likes to talk about
7. Who the character likes to be with
8. How the character's physical appearance affects the way he/she acts

For motives, you should be able to understand from the story what drives the character through the action—what makes the character do what is done. This cannot be put in the text as a statement made by the narrative voice. Your readers will have to figure it out. This part of this exercise can be written as a paragraph. Use the motivation as a topic sentence and in the rest of the paragraph explain why you feel you're right.

You should now create your own character. This might be done in two parts:
1. The actions list
2. The motivations.

The author who wrote the short story you chose went through much of the same process you will be going through, though it may not have been written because of the author's greater experience.

You now should be ready to place your character in a setting. People function differently in different places. You're to decide where your character will appear and describe that place. This should be no more than 800 words and should include the following:
1. Geographic location
2. Time of year
3. Setting (city, small town, farm etc.)
4. The type of house, building, neighborhood

Once you have clearly in mind (and on paper) the place in which your character will operate, you should be ready to create your character sketch.

A character sketch is not a story. It doesn't have a plot or an established structure. It just brings a character alive for the reader. If it's done well, the writer employs the techniques with which you have just had experience. You should do the following in your sketch:
1. Put the character in a place.
2. Let the reader see the character and know what he/she looks like.
3. Have the character interact with people.
4. Have the character function in such a way that the reader understands the motivations behind the acts.
5. Have the character act and react with people and objects.
6. Have the character talk to and listen to other characters.
7. Have the character use his/her body.

You should limit yourself to about 1,500 words.

17

Short Story

Most people, including inexperienced writers, feel that fiction is the easiest kind of writing to do. You know that creative writing is much harder than nonfiction.

You've studied in the past the major elements of short fiction. These, if you employ what you've learned about them, will help you put together a story you can be proud of. There are some things that will help you with this first story if you keep them in mind:

1. Center your story around one character. Have the story develop this character so that the character understands himself or herself better, or so that the reader will understand the character.
2. Keep your time span short. If your story events take place in one hour, it'll be easier to write and will make more sense to your reader than it would if it were to span six months. Also, this will eliminate the problems of major time transitions.
3. Write so that your reader can relate with his senses to what's happening in your story. Stay clear of working with generalizations and abstractions. Use concrete terms whenever possible.
4. Remember that all stories contain conflict. Without this there could be no story.
5. Keep your cast of characters low in number.
6. Let your reader "see" your characters. Don't tell your reader what kinds of people your characters are, let them be developed by having the reader watch them operate in the action of the story.
7. Put your characters in a definite place and time. Your readers must be able to see where your "people" are.
8. Remember that the length limits of short stories will keep you on the task of developing the characters and their problems. There won't be time to write about anything else. Every word you write will have to push your story to its climax. This is what John Gardner calls *profluence*—pushing the story to its conclusion.
9. Write about a problem that you understand. Create characters who are like people you know. Put your story in a place and time you're familiar with.

A final word about "voice". Most books you will find on writing talk about finding your own voice. Boy, is that easy to say. How to do it? I don't know. I don't think people find a voice for writing. Most of us copy in some form the styles of the people we read. Can a person ever have his own style and voice? Maybe, after years of writing.

You'll develop your ear for language as you read, listen and write. You'll develop a style as you practice giving other people your impressions. These experiences will develop your voice.

You might keep this in mind: the only rules that apply to the creative process are those that work for the artist. If you want to break writing rules, do so. The rules are there because they have worked for other people. This doesn't mean they'll work for you.

Any examination of art shows us that much of the really creative work done in painting, sculpting, writing, dance or music broke the rules as they were understood by most people at that time.

One cautionary note. Before you dare break the rules of discourse, you must truly understand them. It's very easy to say you want to shift tenses around when you really don't understand them, and use that as an excuse for not learning the established use. If you want to have fun with authors creating innovative narrative voices (breaking the rules) try reading J. P. Donlevey and Richard Brautigan.

If you want to be a writer, think carefully about the time and effort it will take. For only a few, does success come soon.

But, if you want to write, you will. Nothing will stop you. If you don't want to write, nothing I or any one else can say to you will put your heart in it, and it must be there.

Before you begin to write it might help you to have a clear idea of what the limits and conditions of your story will be. You might find the following note page helpful.

1. The central idea (theme) This could be what some people call your understanding of some aspect of the human condition:

   _____

2. The forces in conflict: _____

   _____

3. The characters who will represent these forces:

   A._____   B._____

4. Time of action: Year:_____ Season:_____Time of Day:_____

5. Location of action: Country:_____State or section:_____

City, town, woods, mountains etc: _____

Characteristics of main characters:

A.   Protagonist: Age:_____ Intelligence:_____Education: _____

Speech Patterns: _____

Attitude toward: Other characters: _____

_____

The conflict or situation: _____

_____

B.   Antagonist: Age:_____ Intelligence:_____Education: _____

     Speech Patterns: _____

Attitude toward: Other characters: _____

_____

The conflict or situation: _____

7.   The action which is the manifestation of the conflict: _____

_____

8.   The incidents in the rising action:

A. _____

_____

B. _____

_____

C. _____

9. The events at the climax:

   A. _____

   _____

   B. _____

   _____

   C. _____

   _____

The resolution of the conflict: _____

_____

_____

_____

11. The symbols used and what they will represent. Many authors maintain that they don't create symbols but they are seen by their readers, but you might be better off planning them:

   A. _____

   B. _____

   C. _____

   D. _____

12. The scenes (the places of the action):

   A. _____

   B. _____

   C. _____

APPENDIX

REWRITING

To show you what rewriting can do for you, I have included three copies of the first paragraph of a paper written by a student in one of my college freshman writing classes.

I have not included the comments I made on the first and second copies. There are still some problems with the third copy, but she had to get on with her paper, and we couldn't spend more time on the introduction.

This is one of the very hard things about learning to write. Your work will never be perfect. Writing is not like doing math. It is never right or wrong. In writing there are only degrees of smoothness or effectiveness. The point when you will have to stop improving a passage and continue with your writing will be one that you can learn only by experience.

You should get in the habit of offering your rough drafts to others who know more than you do about writing. They'll be able to spot things you've missed.

FIRST DRAFT

For centuries storytelling has been a part of life. As children everyone uses stories to explain why something happened. Then as they reach the adult stages of their life the use stories to get a young to sleep or to sooth an upset child. For some adults storytelling is an occupation. These adults, known as authors, choose to spend their time writing their stories down, and making them available for everyone to read.

It's easy to spot problems in this first draft. This student has made no attempt to make this draft perfect. She was just getting her thoughts down on paper. A good way to start.

SECOND DRAFT

For centuries storytelling has been a part of life. As children everyone tells stories to explain why some things happened or how they happened. Then, as they reach the adult stages of their lives, they are stories to put young children to bed or to sooth upset children. For some adults storytelling is an occupation, and they are known as authors. Authors choose to spend their time writing their stories for others to read.

You can see that many of the problems in the first draft are now gone. This copy still is rough, but much improved.

THIRD DRAFT

For centuries storytelling has been a part of life. Children tell stories to explain why things happen or how they happen. Then, as they reach adulthood they tell stories to put children to bed or to sooth upset children. For some adults, storytelling is an occupation, and they are known as authors and choose to spend their time writing.

This draft still has problems, but it's acceptable for the theme she was writing. I have included it in this appendix to show you the process of writing smoothly is not accomplished in the first draft of what a person writes. Smoothness comes from polishing what you've jotted down when it was important to get your ideas on paper.

STUDENT PAPERS GENERATED
BY THESE EXERCISES

#1 Establishing Location for Narrative Voice

Boy on Bike

I was heading north on first, dodging the pot holes with my trusty red Schwinn. Coming closer to the intersection of First and Eagle, on my right, I saw a little old lady (I do mean little) with the biggest Great Dane you've ever seen. That dog was inspecting the fire hydrant at the corner. When the dog saw me he gave a jerk in my direction and the lady let go of the leash. I started to really pedal to get away from that monster. That was when I heard the sirens, and I looked to my left, but the bushes there on the corner got in the way. I couldn't see anything. There was nothing to the right but that lady and her mean dog. Man, I peddled really fast to get across the street—but then there it was. The fire truck. It didn't even slow down. It kept coming, and coming. . .the horn blared and I swerved, and then to keep from hitting the truck, I laid my bike down on its side and we both slid right underneath. Boy, did those rear tires look big when I got that close. I felt the bike hit the far curb and that's the last I remember until that fireman was leaning over me asking me if I was all right.

Old Lady

I saw the whole thing! Or at least what you can see at the south-east corner of Eagle and First, that is. Bruty and I were waiting to cross First when the young man zipped by. I say, if they ever give out tickets for bicycle speeding he'll get one. He was swerving from one side of First to the other, swaying and dodging and no hands at all. Bruty and I were waiting to see where the sirens were coming from, and I called out to the young man—but his head radio was blaring so hard even I could hear it. That's what made Bruty so mad. That boy and his radio scared my dog. Anyway, the boy went right into the intersection, not even slowing down! The fire truck came right through, its brakes were squealing but they couldn't stop, and they collided—the bike disappearing under the truck. I could see a blue car coming east on Eagle, teenagers they were, completely oblivious to the noise of the sirens—and after the boy on the bike slid under the truck, the car must have hit the truck on the other side. I couldn't see the car anymore, but I could tell it hit the truck because of the terrible crash and the truck rocked on its springs. What a mess, I do tell, what a mess.

Boy in Car

Faye was telling me all about the algebra test. (My test is tomorrow.) Karl sat next to Faye and was fiddling with the radio. Karl had the tunes turned up real loud, and with Faye's new speakers, we were having a great time. But anyway, Faye turned from the wheel—only for an instant—to look at me. We were on Eagle and driving up to the west intersection corner of Eagle and First, and I needed to tell her how to get to my house. But then there it was, the fire truck loomed up right in front of us, and I saw a kid on a bike come sliding right under the truck from the other side.
I know I was screaming when we hit.

Fireman

I was right in the middle of telling Mike the instructions; it was an industrial fire and we had to move fast. We were heading south on First and would have to turn right (which is west) on Eagle. When you're in a fire truck it's important to haul those sirens. We used 'em too. I usually wear earmuffs but I forgot. Mike was hanging to the right on Eagle when out of the corner of my eye, I saw that kid come zooming straight through the intersection. Mike saw him too and laid on the horn and pushed the old brakes. But, then I saw that car coming . . .the girl wasn't even looking at us. . .Simultaneously we were hit from both sides. . .the boy slid under us and then the girl's car hit. Her car rocked the whole engine and we were stopped.

Non-involved Voice

As the car travelled eastward on Eagle, it was obvious that those who occupied the vehicle were having a great time. With each bump in the road, the car swerved and bounced, as if in rhythm to its blaring music streaming into the air. She couldn't have been

81

looking or listening for that matter, because when the fire truck on North First Street turned right to go west on Eagle, the car slammed into its side. Then the boy, almost simultaneously sped through the intersection from South First and slid under the fire truck. During the whole thing there was an old lady standing on the corner jumping up and down yelling for her dog that was chasing first the kid on the bike, then the firemen that got out of the truck. That crash really gave the little town of Niles something to talk about.

#2 Further Exercises
in
Establishing Narrative Voice Position

Car Crash

A cool, crisp breath of air drifted through the deep, rich shadows of the sugar maple's leaves, swaying its branches slightly and sending the slender grass of a nearby meadow into a series of ripples that rolled across the field. The sun was almost at its peak and it shone down lazily, glaring off the pavement of the country road that ran by the tree. There was a constant chatter of creatures coming from the meadow which blended with the chirp of crickets and the occasional caw of a crow passing overhead. A bright fleck of red appeared in the tree and then floated to the ground from a lower branch. It was a robin, and it hopped about on the ground trying to catch the vibrations of a grub to give to its young babies that lay waiting in the nest, mouths agape, with an almost impossible hunger. The mother grabbed hold of something in the grass, gave a little tug, and then returned to the nest which was on a branch about four yards from the ground, dropped the squirming meal into a mouth and then returned to the ground to look for another, which she found and gave to a different baby before setting off again toward the earth in search of more food. As she was searching, listening for the underground shaking of her prey, a shrill screech, distant at first but coming closer, echoed from the hills and she returned to her nest.

The driver downshifts as he pulls away from the tight, hairpin curve and begins to accelerate towards the next turn as his bright, red Corvette clings to the roadway, speeding by the countryside which now is nothing but a blur of greens, browns, and blues. He keeps his eyes fixed on the yellow lines running parallel along the edge of the road and he clings to the right side but occasionally swerves over into the other lane. The center dashes have turned into a solid strip now and his hair is blowing wildly in the wind as it rushes over the windshield of his convertible and whips the canvas top which lies folded up behind him. Suddenly, he is upon the curve and he lifts his foot

83

from the accelerator as the car swerves across the center line and into the left lane and then onto the shoulder of the road. He manages to get back on the road again as the engine revs and begins to hum, its pitch getting higher and higher. He is in a straightaway, and even though he almost lost control a moment before, he builds his speed up by flooring the accelerator, 65... 70... 75... 80... 90... 95.... The driver is grasping the steering wheel in a vice-like grip. Then he sees it up ahead. Another curve, tighter than the last one. He doesn't have time to react. He screams as he tries to crank the steering wheel. It's too late. The car spins three times in the center of the road then bounces onto the gravel at the side. The stones spray in a shower in the hot sunlight and the car's front bumper catches in the ditch that runs along the curve in front of the tree. The convertible flips through the air, still going about 80 mph and smashes into the tree with a great SMACK. There is the sound of pieces of the car flying past the tree and landing in the field. . .then nothing. A hubcap slips off the right front tire, rolls a little way, then falls over into a section of the windshield that is lying about twenty-five feet from the car. Greenish-blue antifreeze drips steadily onto a jagged piece of metal that once was the car door, drip. . .drip. . .drip.

The sun was beginning to set low on the horizon and the cloudless sky was slowly becoming darker. Far off in the distance, an old, broken-down windmill appeared to turn by itself for the breeze was no longer blowing. The branches of the trees at the edge of the meadow stood motionless, and the meadow itself was no longer alive with the movements of the little animals that made their homes there. The animals sat quietly, waiting for something to break the silence. Then a chirp of a cricket, and a reply followed, and after that another chirp. Soon there were little chirps and squeals coming from all over the meadow. The rat-tat-tat of a woodpecker in the forest rapped like a distant drum. A red winged blackbird lit on a small sapling in the meadow and ruffled its feathers. A tiny cheep came from the ground near the tree. A baby robin, featherless, and lying on the ground was surrounded by twisted wreckage. Its yellow skin sagged on its tiny skeleton and its wings flapped uselessly as it tried to return to its mother who sat high up in the tree. The mother glided down to the ground and the baby cheeped madly. She scratched the ground a little bit and cocked her head, listening for the vibrations. Hopping a little bit further from the tree, she tilted her head again and immediately plunged her beak into the ground and came up with half a worm. The other half was clinging to its hole desperately. She pulled harder and the worm snapped in two, after which she flew back to the nest to give the meal to a baby before returning to the ground to get another half of the worm to give to her other chick. The sun was almost below the horizon and she went after one more worm before going to the nest for the night.

#3 Senses

Senses

Sight # 1

While I slept the night had peacefully settled. The large, amber colored moon was slowly rising over the leafy roof-like cover of the overhead tree tops. A breeze was picking up making the leaves rustle slightly, for in the night sky clouds were collecting, and a damp feeling was in the air.

Sight # 2

The night had come while I had been sleeping and the sky had turned black with dark clouds. The orange moon that rose full above the tall trees filtered through the twisted and broken branches. The wind that had before shaken those dark old oaks was now dying. A shadowed form stole through the blackness that had settled down around the forest. Mist followed the thing as it wove its way between the trees. The moonlit fog thickened and became so dense I could no longer see the sky or the forest, just the dying embers that lay glowing in the fire pit.

Sound # 1

The library pulsed with voices that mixed together to sound like a group of young children arythmically bashing pans. Screeches filled the room. People yelled across to each other and there was the punctuating thump of books tossed onto table tops. The strident tardy bell cut across the noise and the room settled into silence. The only sounds were an occasional page being turned and the rasp of a light breeze rustling the leaves of a tree by the window.

Sound # 2

The room was full of happy, playful voices that sounded like a river rushing over rapids. People laughed and talked quietly amongst themselves, occasionally raising their voices a bit. But, when the bell rang, the cheerful student voices ceased. Silence settled, and it was so quiet I could even hear the teacher turning the pages of her magazine.

#4 Cheerleader

Cheerleader

The Cheerleader Herself

Point of View:

First person
Attitude subjective
Present tense
Involved
Knowledge limited to participation
Perspective limited to personal view.

I think as I warm up that I'm sure glad Dad and Mom could come and watch me tonight. They have good seats. Even if Mom doesn't like football, I know she always wanted me to be a cheerleader. I can't imagine her doing this when she was younger, but she said she did and really liked it. I bet cheerleading is a lot different now than it was in her day. I look up into the stands and can see some of the gang, and over there, wrapped in a blanket, is Old Lady Franks. I wonder why she comes to these games. I swish my hair around and make one of those halo effects that look so good and think for a bit about Ron. He's so darn cute. I'm glad he came tonight, but not with that Janet. She's not doing him any good at all.

Her Mother

Point of View:

First person plural
Past
Attitude - subjective
Observer Knowledge
perspective restricted to observation

We went to the high school football game Friday evening, and they sure do a wonderful job with the kids there. Everything was so organized, and it all ran so smoothly we were really impressed. That was the first time we have been to one of the games, but we will be

87

going to all of them. It was a very nice experience; all the children were so cute, and they all did such a fine job. We sat in the stands on about the fifty yard line right behind the cheer-leaders. Of course, Janet was there and did a really super job. We were very proud of her. She was by far the best one; of course, she should have been because of all the practice she's done, but then, of course, it's in her genes.

Two Old Men

Point of View.

Third person singular
Past
Objective
Limited omniscient
Omnipresent

John Harbaugh and his neighbor had to step over a number of rows of fans to get to the reserved seats, so there were lots of "Excuse me's," and, "Sorry's." Once seated, Mr. Harbaugh turned to his neighbor and said, "How about a cup of coffee now the game's about to start?"

His neighbor was watching the cheerleaders, and without turning his head, said, "Sure, okay, great." Holding his hand out for the paper cup, he said, "Look at that one on the end. When she twists like that and her hair swirls around her head, it looks just like a halo. Makes me remember when I went here. You know her?"

"Which one?"

"The one on the right end. There, she's looking at us now."

Mr. Harbaugh put the cap back on the thermos and looked down to the field. "Yea, she's a beauty all right. Looks like the one Bill took to the dance last week. I'd sure hate to go through all that again."

At that moment Janet saw an old man in the stands pointing in her direction and thought, "Eat your heart out, old man, you're old enough to be my grandfather!" And as if he could read her mind, Mr. Harbaugh felt embarrassment and looked down at his coffee.

Her Boyfriend

Point of View

First person singular
Future
Subjective
Part of action
Knowledge and perspective restricted

As soon as this dumb game is over I'm gonna get Janet and we can get outa here. Rob is gonna have a great after-game party and none of the jocks'll be there, so I'll have Janet all to myself, and there won't be any of those musclebound guys to give her a rush. First, maybe well stop for a burger and collect some of the gang who didn't go to the game. There oughta be a bunch at the joint and I'll be driving my mom's wagon, so we'll be able to get about fifteen in it. Wow, what a crush. She'll practically have to sit on my lap when I drive. Then we'll make the scene at Rob's, and later, if I don't have to take a whole buncha kids home, we'll have some time alone. I wonder what that'll be like?

Older Lady

Point of View:

First person singular
Subjective
Observer
Knowledge and perspective restricted

I never saw such goings-on. When I was in school we wouldn't think of walking around in such short skirts, much less jumping around like that. These slacks are bad enough. Proper girls should have dresses or skirts that are decent and cover their knees at least.

That one on the end there showing off to the boys in the stands by swinging her hair around like that. If I were her mother, I sure would help her understand what a young lady should act like. I often wonder what the world is coming to. No wonder there's so much trouble nowadays. I bet she saw that kind of thing done by those Texas Cowgirls.

An Objective Narrative Voice

Point of View:

Past
Third person
Objective
Knowledge limited to personal view
Perspective limited to personal view
Not part of action

It was just before the first game of the season. The teams had run onto the field and the stands were full of excited people. The home team bleachers were crammed with students and parents. The stands across the field were about half empty, but those seated were cheering and supporting their team.

The home team cheerleaders were in front of the student section of the stands leading cheers. Janet was on the end, much admired by her boyfriend and her parents, and much envied by most of the girls in the school and even her fellow cheerleaders.

She was whirling and dancing even when the other girls were just standing and talking. She would twirl her long golden hair until it stood straight out, and then she would stop and let her hair wrap around her head. She would have to shake it loose to straighten it.

It looked like she was concentrating on one place in the stands. That may have been where the two older men were pointing at her, or it could have been just behind them where that good looking boy was obviously admiring her.

#5 Truth in the Narrative Voice

The Accident

(C)   The snow hadn't even started falling when Paul and his sister left for the shopping mall. But, as they walked through the exit doors of J.C. Penney's, they stared at the parking lot in amazement. The wind was whipping the snow in what looked like every possible direction as Lisa dashed toward her car and began fumbling in her purse for the keys. Paul, who was five years younger than Lisa, jogged across the nearly deserted parking lot, reaching the passenger door just as Lisa was leaning over to unlock it. He opened the door, grabbed the snow brush and began cleaning off the windshield. Lisa finally got the engine started after three tries, and she honked the horn to make Paul hurry up.

(A)   The snow was really coming down when Lisa and I walked out of that mall. At least six inches were already on the ground, and I remember thinking, "Lisa is really gonna get nailed when we get home." It didn't bother me too much, I knew I wouldn 't get yelled at. I wasn't the one who insisted we go to the mall even though the weatherman was forecasting blizzard conditions. It was so hard to see anything that night with all the snow flying everywhere. It was an adventure to just get out of the parking lot. We had almost made it when I saw that car stuck in a snow bank. I didn't really hesitate to get out and try to help. For all I knew there could have been a seventy year old lady in that car, and since there weren't very many cars left in the parking lot, there was no telling how long she'd have to wait before somebody else came along.

(B)   I was in one big hurry that night, and my wife, Gladys, kept telling me to slow down. I really hate it when she tells me how to drive. She knows how her yelling makes me angry, but she goes right ahead and does it anyway. I just wanted to get away from the mall and go home. How I hate Christmas shopping! Hey, don't think that that accident was my fault, though. I wasn't driving like some crazy lunatic.

91

(C) Paul was positioned behind the rear bumper of Mrs. Woodson's car. It only took a minute or so of rocking to get the wheels unstuck. Mrs. Woodson rolled down her window and thanked Paul for his help. she offered him money and was obviously sincerely grateful, but he refused and told her to be careful going home. She nodded and thanked him again as she pulled away. Paul watched her for a moment just to make sure she didn't get stuck again, then he turned around just in time to see the blue Datsun. Even though the driver had slammed on the brakes, there was no way Paul could get out of the car's path quickly enough, and the bumper smacked into his legs, throwing him into a somersault. He landed in a spread-eagle position, sprawled across the hood, as Lisa, who saw the whole thing, screamed and covered her eyes.

(A) I honestly didn't know what hit me. I remember seeing a blue flash and then it felt like I got tackled by a two hundred and fifty pound linebacker. It was just like in the movies when they show the action scene in slow motion to make it more dramatic. I recall flying for a split second and then having the wind knocked out of my lungs. Then, everything was quiet for a few seconds. I rolled off the hood and stood up as the driver opened his door.
   "You okay, kid?" he asked, his eyes wide.
   "Yeah, I think so." I was pretty scared at the time.
   "Good. I'm sorry about that," he said, as he got back in the Datsun. I watched as he drove off in a hurry.

(B) I saw the kid the whole time. He looked at me and I figured he was going to let me drive by first. But, then he did the craziest stunt and stepped right out in front of my car. What was I supposed to do? I didn't have any traction on that snow, and there was no way I could stop. I think he just wanted to scare me or something. Well, I let him know he didn't get the best of me. He had a pretty scared look on his face, but I could see through his little joke. I wasn't gonna let some punk kid fool me into thinking I'd really hurt him.
   I barely bumped him and he goes flying on top of the hood like he'd been shot or something. I let him know he didn't fool me. It took a while for me to calm Gladys down.

92

#6 Dramatic Dialogue

Scene From, "Is Love a Four Letter Word ?"

Elizabeth is a fifteen year-old girl who has two, very career-minded parents. She is at the stage in her life when she needs attention and love from them, but they are too wrapped up in their business affairs to notice. So, she has run away.

Setting: A bus terminal in Chicago, 3:00 a.m., on a Wednesday in January. Elizabeth is sitting on a bench (center stage) wrapped in a ski jacket. Her arms are folded across her chest in a manner which indicates she is very cold. A suitcase rests at her feet. Her head is bobbing as if she is trying to stay awake but keeps falling asleep. Two bums are sleeping on benches located in each corner upstage. A policeman enters from stage left, looking disgustedly at the bum (left) who is snoring loudly. He holds a baton in his right hand and is hitting it gently against the palm of his left hand. He sees Elizabeth and walks over to her bench. He stands behind the bench, looking down at her. Elizabeth senses the policeman's presence and wakes up, startled.

E: Hi. (nervously)
P: Late departure, eh?
E: (Blinking eyes, trying to wake up) Yea, four thirty. (Yawning and stretching) I wanted to be sure I didn't miss it.
P: (Walks around the bench and sits down next to her.) What's your name?
E: Elizabeth. Elizabeth Roberts. (She clears her throat.)
P: Are you going to visit relatives, Elizabeth?
E: Yes, my grandma. (She blurts it out then looks down at her feet.) She's all alone and . . .well, very ill.
P: (He looks around the station.) Didn't your parents even wait to see you off?
E: Yea, they. . .My bus got delayed, though.
P: Oh, I've heard the buses and trains have been running late on account of the storm. So, where are you headed ?
E: Missouri.
P: No kidding! That's where I'm from. Where about in

Missouri?

E: (She pauses. She obviously hasn't considered where exactly she wanted to go.)
Umm. . .Little Rock! (She frowns and sinks down into the bench, realizing what she has said.)

P: Ahh? Little Rock, Missouri. Can't say I've heard of it, but it's a big state. (He has caught on to the mistake but continues to play along) It's beautiful countryside there.

E: Uh huh. (Not looking up.)

P: (He turns his head toward her.) How old are you, Elizabeth?

E: Eighteen, last month.

P: Boy you don't look that old. Where do you live?

E: (Looking at him) Yea, my mother says that's a good quality to have. . .not looking as old as I really am, I mean. (She speaks enthusiastically, trying to change the subject.) I figure, when I'm forty, I'll only look thirty-five and that way I'll feel much younger than I am. I guess it's 'cause I'm so active in school, ya know? I play volleyball, I'm in student council and drama club.

P: (He nods, then says patiently.) Why don't I take you home so you can wait for the bus with your folks. It's a real blizzard outside, and your bus is probably stuck at some other station anyway.

E: (Sighing.) No, I have to catch my bus. (Pointing.) That guy, over there, said it would be here at four.

P: Really, Elizabeth, this bus station isn't safe for a young girl alone, at this hour. C'mon, I'll take you home. (He stands up.) I wouldn't feel right leaving you here by yourself.

E: No. No, thanks. I'll wait. I really do have to see my grandma. (Sadly.) She could go any day now.

P: Well, you can catch a bus tomorrow, can't you? I'm sure your parents wouldn't want you to spend the night in a bus station.

E: Yes they would! (Loudly.)

P: (Calmly) Well, let's call them and find out. (He starts to walk toward a pay phone, stage right.)

E: (Running over in front of him.) No, I'm sure they're asleep now. Look, thanks for your consideration, I really appre-ciate you being nice to me and all, but-

P: Okay, young lady, (Taking her arm) this little game is over. You're going home, now.

E: (She pulls away from him.) Just leave me alone.

I know my rights. I'm an adult.

P: Eighteen years old, right? Okay then, what year were you born? Quick!

E: Nineteen hundred and sixty three. (He shakes his head.) Sixty two?

P: Let's go. (Taking her by the arm again.)

E: Oh, all right. (She turns to pick up her suitcase. He lets go of her arm.)

P: Where do you live?

E: 3682 Tarquin Avenue. (Stepping toward him)

P: Here, (reaching for the suitcase.) let me carry that for you.

E: No, that's okay. I can manage. (They exit left.)

#7 Reader Reaction

Canoe Trip

Jimmy Peters watched as his father, seated in the stern of the canoe, pushed off from shore with his aluminum paddle. The canoe drifted with the current toward the middle of the Great Bear River and Jimmy clung to the side of the boat and stared wide-eyed as the black, swift-running water streamed by. "Dad, I don't like it. Take me back," he murmured through tight lips.

"We just got started, give it a chance. Here," his father said, handing him a paddle, "take this and watch how I do it." His father picked up his own paddle from the canoe bottom and adjusted his grip on it until it felt comfortable. "Put one hand on this end and the other about halfway down like me."

Jimmy clumsily took hold of the paddle and tried to adjust his hands as his father had done. "Like this?"

"Yea, but just relax. Pretend it's a baseball bat. Now, you don't row with a canoe paddle, you dig." He demonstrated, dipping the paddle into the water ahead of him and pulling with his strong shoulders and arms, keeping the handle steady until it was stretched out behind him.

Jimmy attempted the same thing his dad had done, but as he dipped the paddle into the water, the strong current wrenched it from his small hands. Reaching over the edge, his father was able to grab it before it drifted away. "You have to hold on tight!" he exclaimed.

"I'm sorry. I didn't know the current was so strong."

"Well, you do now. Here, try it again." He handed him the paddle.

Jimmy grabbed it and placed his hands in the correct position, then dipped the paddle into the water and pulled. The canoe glided through the water with a little more speed.

"That's it, now you've got it. See if you can switch sides."

Jimmy readjusted his hands and dipped the paddle on the starboard side. He pulled and the canoe picked up speed again. "Oh, wow."

"Now you paddle on the right side and I'll paddle

on the left."

After a couple of hours they both began to get tired and decided to take a break for lunch.

"What's that sound?" Jimmy asked as he chewed up a bite of bologna sandwich.

"I think it's just the wind or something," his father said, gulping a swallow of pop.

"It keeps getting louder, I thought maybe it was. . .look!" Jimmy pointed up ahead where the water had suddenly become rough.

"Quick head for shore, it's a waterfall!" Mr. Peters lunged for his paddle, spilling the contents of his pop can in his lap. The canoe flipped suddenly under the weight shift and Jimmy screamed. His father, trying to regain his balance, leaned too far to one side and the canoe capsized. Jimmy surfaced first, struggling and splashing. He tried to yell but only succeeded in catching a wave of water in his mouth. The life jacket tied about his neck kept him bobbing like a bright orange cork, but it did not stop him from getting dangerously close to the waterfall, which roared in his water-filled ears, the strong pull of water drawing him closer every moment. He searched the river behind him, desperately looking for his father, and finally caught sight of the other life jacket. But something was wrong. His father wasn't floating like he should have been; his face was almost completely submerged, and his arms were sprawled out. He didn't move.

Jimmy started to cry. He turned his head and looked up ahead at the falls just in time to see the aluminum canoe tilt over the edge. He kicked his feet wildly and clawed at the water, but it was too late. Suddenly he felt the water drop out from beneath him, and his body tumbled thirty-five feet and then splashed into the frothy water at the bottom of the falls. He was tugged at and jerked about under the surface as if he were a doll. Unable to see anything in the dark, muddy water, his lungs began to ache and he clawed at the water in an effort to reach air. His head broke the surface and he gasped, choking on a mouthful of water. The swirling current pulled at his legs and he was yanked beneath again. He was thrown against a jagged boulder, the remaining air was forced from his lungs and he felt his right arm snap on the impact. In a final attempt to save himself Jimmy reached out with his left hand for something, anything to pull himself up. His head hurt but his arm was numb, and he wished there was someone he could yell to for help, but he knew there was no one within fifty miles except his father who floated lifelessly somewhere above the falls.

Then his hand brushed against something and he grasped it. Feeling the smooth, round, texture of a tree root, he held on with a vice-like grip but the current pulled his body and he could feel his hand slowly slipping off. Forcing his head above the frothing water, he took one last breath and then let go. He drifted down, kicking with his legs for a while, then simply floating with the flow. He felt the ache in his lungs again, but this time he did not try to swim to the surface, for he had given up. A few more seconds and he would breathe in the muddy water and it would all be over.

Think! His head slammed into something hard. It was a log sticking out into the river, half-submerged.

Jimmy reached up with his good arm and wrapped it around the slimy trunk. This new hope gave him a burst of extra strength and in one mighty heave, he swung his leg up onto the log. Straining, he got the other up too, and he was out of the water. He lay on his stomach +and tried to catch his breath.

This last effort had sapped all of Jimmy's strength and he was completely exhausted. His eyes began to get heavy and close when something brushed against his ear. Twisting his neck to see what it was, he came face to face with a shiny black water moccasin, tensed and ready to attack

Jimmy only had time to scream as it struck the huge fangs hitting him right below the chin piercing his neck. Jimmy grabbed the muscular body and pulled the fangs out of his throat and flung the snake out into the river. He clawed frantically to get off of the tree and up on the bank but the last thing he saw before he sank to his death was the snake swimming past him.

#8 Symbols in Literature

Lost in the Woods

The sun was beginning to peek up over the trees. In a few minutes it was shining through the leaves and into Todd and Shawn's bedroom window waking both of them. They lay in their soft beds covered with the large quilts their mother had made them for Christmas. Both were tired since they had stayed up so late talking and watching television the night before, so they stayed in bed for awhile, chatting. Soon, from downstairs, their mother called to them. "Shawn, Todd, breakfast."

Todd said, "Great, I'm starvin."

"Oh, me too, man," said Shawn. They jumped out of bed, got dressed and ran downstairs. They could hardly wait to eat. The scent of coffee filled the kitchen along with the smells of bacon and pancakes. It was very warm in the kitchen thanks to the new wood stove their father had built and installed the day before.

The whole family sat at the dining room table for breakfast that day as they did on every Sunday, father at the head of the table.

"What are you boys going to do today?" asked their father.

Todd quickly replied, "We'd really like to go out in the woods for a while."

"Yea, to pick berries. So mom can bake a pie for dessert tomorrow night," Shawn added.

"That's a good idea," said father. "But remember, you are not to go across the creek. It's too dangerous."

"We won't," both boys said in unison. Todd looked across the table to Shawn with his face down towards his plate. They both knew the plan was to sneak across anyway.

Their parents told them they would be going out of town that night and for them to walk over to Mrs. Boone's. She had been told they might be over to stay the night.

"Be sure to pack your overnight bags and take them with you to the woods in case we aren't here when you get back because the house is going to be locked, and I don't want you here alone," said their mother.

After they had finished their second helping of the

delicious breakfast, the boys went upstairs to clean their room and pack their bags for the night.

"Are you sure we should do this, Todd?" Asked Shawn.

"Heck ya," said Todd. "Aren't you curious about what it's like on the other side of the river?"

"Of course. But I don't wanna get in trouble," said Shawn.

"Don't worry," said Todd. "Mom and dad are gonna be out of town all night, and Mrs. Boone doesn't even know for sure we're coming. She won't until we get there."

When they were ready to go, they told their parents they were heading for the woods right then. Their mom and dad each gave them a kiss and a hug and reminded them to behave themselves for Mrs. Boone.

They walked through the woods with their bags and chopped at the branches that were in their way with their jackknives.

They talked about the river constantly until they reached it. On this side it was easy to walk and to find the berry bushes. There was long grass but mostly the ground was clear. They could see across the narrow river, and the bank was high on that side. The trees and bushes grew close to the bank. There didn't seem to be any good places to cross. And even if they could get across they weren't sure they could get up the far bank.

They began looking for berries, but they couldn't find any good ones that weren't dried up.

"There aren't any good berries here," said Todd with a grin.

"Nope, better go across the river and see if there are some better ones over there," said Shawn. They prepared for this trip by dressing in their boots and thermal socks. They got to the river and walked through the brown knee-high water as they laughed and talked. The bottom was full of weeds and mush and they laughed about the suction noises they made with their boots.

It was a real job getting up the bank onto the far side of the river. Here the trees grew close together and cut out most of the sunlight. Trees hung out over the river and made it very spooky. Shawn got pretty scared when Todd began teasing him about swamp creatures and killers in scary movies, and he started to cry a little.

They had forgotten about berries. They were more interested in looking for old knives, rocks, salamanders, dead animals and all the things boys like to play with. They spent most of that day searching the forbidden woods. At one point they stopped and ate the sandwiches their mother had prepared for them. When they first noticed that the sun was getting lower in the sky, the boys decided they better head for Mrs. Boone's.

It was then that they realized they had no idea which way to go. They had been walking around all day and had gotten lost. They could find no signs of where they had been. It soon was very dark since the sun was setting and they were surrounded by trees. As it grew black, the boys became exhausted to the point they could hardly walk. They picked a soft, dry, grassy spot under a maple tree and sat and talked. There were strange noises in the woods. Todd reached out his hand and found his brother's. The wings of a large bird made a loud fluttering near them and they both jumped, then laughed at themselves.

In a short while they were both asleep.

Birds began chirping as the sky lightened in the east and Shawn woke up suddenly. "Todd, wake up. We fell asleep. We slept here all night. Oh, my gosh, we gotta find our way home before mom and dad get home," Shawn said frantically.

They picked up their bags and started walking again in the still dark woods. In about an hour they spotted a light. They thought it could be their home and headed for it. They soon came to the river and walked once again through the brush and down into the water.

When they got closer to the light they could tell it was coming from their kitchen window. Figures were moving in the kitchen. They knew they had found their home where they belonged.

"Thank goodness we found it," said Shawn.

"I knew we would all the time," said Todd calmly.

They walked to the back door and then realized they were wet from the knees down and were very muddy from sliding down the bank. They looked at each other and Shawn said, "We gotta tell the truth."

"Of course we do," answered Todd. "Don't we always?"

#9 Identification and Symbolism
in an
Extended Flashback

The Kite

As Lynn carried a box out to the car she called to her husband, "Phil, while I put these things in the trunk, could you close all the windows?"

"Sure, Honey," answered Phil. His footsteps echoed strangely throughout the empty house as he walked from room to room, slamming shut windows and checking for boxes left behind. The carpet and furniture, which had once given the house a feeling of warmth and security, were packed away. Phil saw a box in the corner of Joey's room, and as he bent to pick it up, noticed it contained a pair of binoculars. While carrying that last box of toys outside, Phil recalled the day he and Joey had visited Pa Tom's farm. They had tramped through the woods together using the binoculars to identify many different species of birds. The thought occurred to Phil, not for the first time, that never again would they share an afternoon. A feeling of grief and loss made him feel weak and sick to his stomach.

After dropping the box in the trunk, Lynn looked back for a final time at the house. Her gaze shifted to the large, old maple tree, its limbs bare against the cloudy November sky. She saw the kite with the broken ribs and faded colors high up in the branches. Its tail was wrapped around the electrical wires, and a stray piece of broken twine hung from a bare tree branch. Memories of Joey came back to her, especially that one day many months ago when he had come running into the house after school, talking excitedly about Ben's newest toy.

Joey had wanted a kite just like Ben's, but Joey's kite would fly twice as high and look twice as beautiful high up in the clear March sky. Joey's father had taken him to the toy store that evening, and upon returning home, Joey proudly showed off his kite.

"See Mommy, we got the last blue one they had. Isn't it neat, huh, isn't it?"

"Let's put it together now," said his father, "and maybe we can fly it tomorrow."

Joey raced around the house collecting tape and glue while his mother found an old sheet which would make a long tail. Before bed that night the kite was finished, and when Joey woke the next morning it lay on the kitchen table, ready to be flown.

After only two false starts Joey's kite was swaying and diving in the sky.

"Daddy, how come my kite can stay up in the sky, but, when I jump up, I can't?"

"Well, Joey, your kite is a lot lighter than you are, and it was made a special way so it could fly." His father pulled a piece of paper and a pen out of his pocket and drew a diagram, explaining the law of gravity and how air currents helped the kite to fly.

"Phil," called Joey's mother, "the washer isn't working, and it's spilled water all over the utility room floor. Can you come and take a look at it?"

"Okay, I'll be inside in a minute." He started across the lawn toward the house. "Can you keep your kite in the air while I help your mom?"

"Yeah, Dad," Joey called to his father as he turned back to his kite.

"Come on, kite, you can fly higher, I know you can. Even Ben's kite flies higher than this." Joey let out too much string, though, and the kite began to dive slightly. He ran across the yard, trying to pull his kite out of the dive, but instead tripped and fell down. The string went slack in Joey's hand, and he looked up just in time to see it crash into the top of the maple tree. "Dad. . .Daddy. . .Daddy!" yelled Joey, but no one answered.

After picking himself up off the ground, Joey looked at the maple tree, which had several limbs growing quite close to the ground, and he decided he could climb to his kite himself. He jumped up and grabbed hold of a branch. Using his feet to scale the trunk of the tree, Joey was soon sitting on one of its lower limbs. He then reached to the branch above him and repeated the process, shinning a knee once when his foot slipped. He climbed higher and until finally the kite was within reach. While eagerly stretching to grasp it, he lost his balance and fell onto the electrical wires that ran along the road in front of his house. Hundreds of volts of electricity shot through his body and Joey dropped to the ground.

"Joey, Joey, are you all right?" cried his father when he saw his son lying on the ground under the tree. He and his wife ran to his body.

"Oh, dear Lord in Heaven," cried his mother, while his father bolted into the house to call the hospital.

103

Soon an ambulance raced up the street, sirens screaming, drawing neighbors from their homes to the sidewalk to watch. The agile young men in white coats lifted Joey onto a stretcher and placed him in the ambulance. Phil put his arm around Lynn, and tears ran down her face as the ambulance was driven back down the street. The sirens were silent; there was no need for them.

"Phil, Phil, our baby is dead," sobbed Lynn as she ran to their car.

"Maybe not," shouted Phil, as he started the car to follow the ambulance. "Maybe not."

Lynn slammed down the trunk lid and climbed into the car. Phil started the engine, and, as they drove off down the street, it began to rain. That night the wind blew down the few remaining leaves from the maple tree, and with them came the kite. It ended up in Mrs. Peterson's yard, and the next day Joey's kite was added to a smoldering pile of leaves.

#10 Creating Mood

Mood

Kate looked out the window of her 42nd floor apartment in the middle of downtown New York. She thought of her twin brother, Alan, and how much she missed him. They had been so close as children, and now after his death she felt as if she had lost half of herself. She thought back to the golden days of their childhood when everything seemed perfect. She remembered the countless summers they had spent at their grandparents' house.

Together, the two of them swam in the river, explored the swamps that surrounded the area, and climbed the trees. Kate and Alan had even built a clubhouse in the giant oak tree which stood in the front yard. This was their own little world where no one was allowed to enter. All of their secrets, ideas, and most prized possessions, everything they had, were shared between the two of them.

"Why did he have to give up on life?" Kate wondered aloud. It had hurt her to think that Alan hadn't come to her to talk things out before he committed suicide. She thought of last month when their mother had called and told her of Alan's death.

"He hung himself Katherine," her mother had sobbed over the phone.

Kate felt hot tears on her cheeks and realized she was crying. She wiped her face with the back of her hand and looked down at the street. The cars moved along like a huge army of ants marching to some destination of their own.

"What a dreary day," she thought as she looked at the gray misty sky which hung gloomily over the city. She gave a startled jump as her cat, Chester, pounced up on the window sill.

Oh, it's you. You shouldn't scare me like that, Chester. Hey, how would you like to get out of this place for a while? We're going to drive out to Gram and Gramp's old house for the weekend. It'll do us good to get some fresh air for a change."

The cat dropped to the floor and curled up in a ball near the heater. Kate packed a few things in a small suitcase. When she was done, it was nearly noon, but the gray light coming in through the windows made it look more like early in the evening. In the odd light the apartment looked drab, dismal, and lonely. Kate fought off feelings of depression as she picked up her suitcase, the cat and some cat food and groceries for herself.

"I've just got to get out of here," she said to herself. This place is really getting to me. "She kicked the door shut with her foot, set Chester down to make sure the door was locked, picked him up again, and then walked down the hallway towards the elevator.

When Kate stepped outside, the sharp chill of the air hit her. She ran to her car, a small green Volvo, and unloaded her things in the back seat. Chester jumped into the front seat on the passenger's side and settled down for a nap. Kate pulled out into the street. It was a four or five hour drive up to the house, so she had a long way to go.

She stopped for a red light and looked at the skyscrapers that loomed up all around her. She felt trapped and caged in. The gray walls of the buildings blotted out everything except for a few patches of colorless sky.

"So this is New York, the Big Apple, the city where everyone's dreams are supposed to come true," she thought as she looked at the litter-lined gutters and a wino who sat in an alley trying to get warm.

The light turned green and Kate started off. She wanted to be free from the city before the buildings closed in on her.

Kate finally reached the open highway that led out of the city. Many other cars, mostly large trucks, were headed out as well. The road that went back into New York was locked in a traffic jam, and Kate was thankful that she could leave the smog and congestion behind. As she drove, the signs of the city thinned out and the trees, grass, and farmhouses clearly showed she was now in the country. Kate felt better. The air was fresh and the sun shone brightly. Chester, who had awakened but was uninterested in this new scenery, settled himself back down and went to sleep again.

The Volvo pulled onto the dirt road that went to the house. To Kate's left was a dense forest, and to her right was a wide stream that ran parallel to the road. After driving about two miles, Kate could see the house. A smile flashed across her face. "This is home," she said, "Home."

She made a turn to the right and crossed the

rickety old bridge that arched above the stream. She
parked the car and went off to explore. She looked at
the house with its fallen-off shutters, peeling paint,
and rotted steps. Her eyes swept over the yard and the
tall grasses, weeds, and tangled bushes.

The swamp curved around the back and sides of the
house, and an old tire swing hung by a few threads of
remaining rope. Kate shut her eyes and thought of what
the house used to look like. Bright and cheery with
freshly cut grass and lots of people around.

She looked up at the sky and noticed some storm
clouds were rolling in and had already covered the sun.
She got her things out of the car and climbed the steps
to the front door. The wooden boards creaked, and when
she opened the door, it squeaked on its rusty hinges.
Once in the hallway, Kate flicked on the light switch,
but nothing happened.

"Of course, no electricity," she said aloud.

She turned right into the kitchen and foraged
around for some candles. She found an old red one in
one of the drawers. She pulled out some matches from
her pocket and lit it. She walked over to the old hand
pump in a corner of the sink set down the candle, and
pushed down the handle with all her might. The dust and
cobwebs flew up and the handle gave way with a great
creaking sigh. After a few more pumps, rusty water
poured out, but it soon turned clear.

"Well, at least I'll have water," she thought to
herself.

She carried the candle into the living room across
the hallway. All of the furniture was coated in dust,
and every once in a while a cockroach hurried over the
floor trying to evade the glow of light.

She went over to the window and looked out. The
first few raindrops were beginning to fall from the
black clouds that hung overhead. She turned away from
the window to continue her look around the room. In the
corner next to the window sat the baby grand piano
which had once been black and shiny with ivory keys,
but now the wood was splintered, and the polish gone.
Some of the keys were even missing. She sat down on the
bench and remembered how her grandmother had played and
sung while she and Alan had sat and listened en-
thralled with the music.

"Sing some more for us, Gram."

"Okay, Alan. What do you want to hear?"

"How about Twinkle Twinkle Little Star?"'

"All right. Do you want to hear that one too,

107

Katie?"

"Yes, please, Gram."

Then the two of them would sit and clap their hands or do little dances in time to the music.

Suddenly Kate heard a scratching at the front door. When she opened it, Chester walked in and shook himself off in the hallway. He was soaked.

"Oh, you poor kitty. Did I leave you out in the rain? I'm sorry."

She picked him up and began drying him off. Then she looked out the window by the door. It was nearly dark now, but she could still see the rain pouring down in sheets.

"This is going to be a big one," she said to Chester. "Come on, I'll get you some cat food."

Just then Kate heard a crash out in the front yard. When she looked out, she could just barely see the wreckage of the old bridge being carried off down the stream.

"Now we're stranded here and the Gibson's live a good two miles away," she said to Chester. "I guess we'll just have to wait it out until morning."

She walked into the living room and sat down. Chester followed her and jumped into her lap. It was pitch black outside now, but the rain continued to fall. There was also an occasional flash of lightning followed by the sound of thunder.

"I know, I'll start a fire," Kate said aloud as she looked at the old fireplace. "How stupid of me not to think of it sooner."

She got up, built the fire, and soon had it going. It cast an eerie glow over the room and shadows danced and flickered on the walls.

"I'm so glad to be here," she said to Chester, who now lay before the fireplace. "It was a good idea after all." She settled back down in her chair and was soon asleep.

When Kate awoke, the fire was almost out and the cat had disappeared. She was startled to hear scraping noises at the windows and then realized it must be the bushes that had grown up beside the house. She was on her way to the kitchen when she heard sniffling noises at the front door as if a dog were trying to get in.

"Oh, you've got a wild imagination," she said to herself "Now just you stop it."

As the night wore on the noises increased. When she stood near the front door she could follow the sniffling noises as they traveled up the cracks where the door met the jam. When they reached the top of the door, she realized that whatever it was outside trying to smell at the door was very big, and she retreated to a chair in the corner of the living room, not even daring to make a sound.

She had a candle in her hand which gave a weak light. She had been staring out the window on the other side of the room when suddenly a huge furry body pressed up against the glass and then was quickly gone. Kate offered a small cry and ran upstairs to the bedroom she and Alan had shared as children. There she found Chester curled up on one of the beds. She hugged him and lay down on the bed and fell asleep again.

Kate woke up to a bright sunny day. Light streamed in through the windows and birds chirped outside. She went down to the kitchen and began to fix breakfast. She set out some cat food for Chester, and after she was done eating, walked outside to check the damage. The front door didn't have any scratches on it that she could see. The stream raged and bubbled. The rain had caused water to overflow the banks, and there was no way she could wade across or even swim because of the swiftly moving current. Then she walked around the side of the house to look at the windows. The bushes were high, but not high enough to scrape the window panes. "It was probably the rain then," she thought.

The swamp that surrounded part of the house was noticeably higher, but not enough to cause any damage. Except for the ruined bridge, some fallen tree branches , and a few more shutters that had come off, everything seemed to be in order. Kate went over to look at the tire swing. She was glad to see it had lasted through the storm.

Alan used to push her as high as he could until she got scared, and then he would let Kate push him. He loved going high up in the air, but it terrified Kate. She laughed bitterly as she thought, "Oh, what I wouldn't give to have him push me now until I screamed." She then walked back into the house to look for Chester.

Night came quickly and Kate made another fire. She sat with the cat on her lap sleeping peacefully. All was quiet outside, but as the hours passed, she began to hear the scraping at the windows. The noises at the door turned from sniffs to grunts and snorts. She walked to the door to follow the noise again. Chester had jumped off her lap and had retreated to the kitchen. Kate put her hands on the door and could feel a pressure as if something was trying to push it in. She heard a vicious clawing and snarling and felt the wood of the door being splintered apart. She ran to the upstairs bedroom and shut the door. She heard a wet sucking noise at the window and saw again the dark fur press against the glass. Her piercing screams echoed through the rooms.

Downstairs the fire crackled and Chester lay nearby, comfortable in the heat from the fire.

Sheriff Baker pulled up on the dirt road and looked over at the old Cranston house. He was out checking for flood damage from the storm. He saw Kate's car parked on the island that had formed after the bridge had fallen and decided to go see if everything was okay. He got his small rowboat off the trailer and set it in the stream. Once across the water he tied the boat to a small tree that stood in a foot of water. When he got to the steps he saw that a brown and white cat was sitting in front of the door, swinging its tail back and forth and purring slightly.

"Hi there, kitty," the sheriff said as he bent down and patted the cat on the head. Then he stood up and started to open the front door but stopped to take a closer look and ran his hand along the wooden panels.

"Hello," he called out, but nobody answered. He searched the bottom floor and then went upstairs. He looked through several rooms on the right side of the hallway, and then checked out a bedroom on the opposite side.

When he opened the door of the closet he was horrified. "Oh my, what happened?" he asked, as he looked down at Kate curled up in a fetal position in the closet. Her arms were wrapped protectively around her and her knees were tight against her chest.

"Ma'am, can I help you? What's wrong? What happened?"

When Kate gave no answer, he gently picked her up and carried her out of the house. The cat followed and jumped into the rowboat with them. The sheriff laid Kate down in the boat. She remained motionless, her body curled in a tight ball.

#11 Satire

In Spite for Us

I had been attending Niles Academy for about two months when I first heard of orals. It was in October, the year the Russians completed their first space station. I had come in after school to talk to my compu-counselor about my schedule, and when I rounded the corner to the science hall, I found myself in the middle of about 150 students staring at thick bundles of papers and mumbling quietly to themselves, eyes glazed. I was startled, to say the least, and stepped off the autotrack to find out just what was going on.

"Hello, " I said to a girl I knew only as Lisa, sitting against the hallway wall, head bent over very worn sheets of printed paper. She didn't respond, so I tapped her on the shoulder.

"Methemalbumenia " she yelled, her head shooting up to face me.

"Excuse me?" I asked, trying to figure out what she had said.

"Oh, oh, I'm sorry," she said. "It's just that you startled me. I was, am, studying."

"Studying?" I asked. "Is that what all these people are doing?"

"Yes, that and waiting," she replied. "We're taking our biology orals."

Suddenly, the classroom door behind me burst open and a student stormed out, cussing and looking very angry. As the door began to swing shut I peered inside and saw another fifty or so students, acting in the same manner as those in the hall.

As a student shoved his way through the crowd, I asked, "What's wrong with him?"

"Oh, that's Adam. He's been here every night for as long as anyone can remember. He just got inside today. I guess he didn't pass them." She looked back down at her paper and resumed mumbling to herself.

I was still confused. "Hasn't passed what? I don't understand."

"Orals, orals!" She thrust the bundle of papers into my face. "These are orals. Mr. Quack he's our teacher, gives us these definitions every six weeks. We study them and he quizzes us on them individually. If we miss one, we go to the end of the line and do it over again."

I looked over the single spaced, computer printed paper in front of me. "It looks pretty tough."

"Yea, I guess, " Lisa said. "There's about nine hundred definitions, eighteen pages."

I looked at her in disbelief. "That sounds impossible! You must have a lot of chances to get them."

"Well, not really. With all these people, we get two, maybe three chances at the most, and that's if we come here every night for a few hours to wait in line." She looked back down at her paper.

The classroom door opened again and another student walked out, sobbing quietly. A loud, maniacal laugh emanated from the back of the room, startling me. "What was that?" I asked.

Lisa looked up from her paper. "That was Mr. Quack our teacher."

"Sounds like he's having fun," I said as a student elbowed past me and entered the room.

"Oh, he really enjoys giving orals. He almost never leaves his room. In fact, now that I think about it, I've never seen him leave." She was silent for a moment. "I've heard he's married, but I don't know how. . ."

The crowd of students seemed to be pressing closer and closer to the door, making me a little nervous. Another unhappy student exited the room.

"Well, Lisa, I've got to go. I hope you get them, I said, as I started to push my way out of the crowd, catching a few of the foreign-sounding words the students were mumbling. I didn't understand any of them.

"Good afternoon, Mr. Paul," the compu-counselor said, when I finally found it. "Here is your new schedule. First hour, English - Wilson. Second hour, chemistry - Baker. Third hour, Biology - Quack. . ."

"No! It can't be!" I screamed to the monitor. Of course it couldn't hear me, and when I typed in the instruction, Clarify, it replied, "Clarify - elucidate, (Antiphrasis) Obfuscation."

#12 Using Tenses

Love of Nature

The grass is covered with dew this morning, and as I walk quickly through the sun-sprinkled field, with my collection jar in my hand, my shoes and pants are just as quickly becoming as wet as the grass and weeds already are. I am almost to the place where I planned to come, and I am becoming increasingly excited. I can see, at the bottom of the hill and around the corner, the hilly tree-surrounded, secluded beginning of the steep-trailed incline.

Running down the hill on that sunny fall day, I was so happily overwhelmed with the feeling of monotony and the excellence of the day. The leaves were beautifully blended with yellow, orange, brown, and fiery red colors, and they were still hanging on firmly to their branches. I was happy at that, because the sun wouldn't lighten the trail my feet were following, it would only dance all around me, keeping as much to itself as I was.

I carried a big, empty, glass jar which once contained Jiffy Peanut Butter. The jar remained empty for a while; I didn't feel like catching strange insect specimens to take home yet. I had to finish soaking up the day's glorious start as I walked up the steep incline.

I have two different spiders in my jar. One's a daddy long leg and I don't know what the other one is, but he has a hairy body and hairy legs. They were attacking each other when they just met a few minutes ago. There goes one of daddy's legs!

I love these little critters, I love these surroundings, and I love life! I see a boxer turtle walking slowly across the trail in front of me and I run to pick it up. He's one of the biggest boxers I've seen for quite some time.

I saw three that morning. I was so fascinated. Three of them, each different from the others. A mommy, a daddy, and a baby. I wanted so badly to take them home with me, but I wasn't finished exploring, learning; and I wouldn't be able to carry them and my jar also. So, I let each of them go its own way.

I walked on until I came to my resting place; a fallen tree to the side of the trail. A giant grasshop

113

per jumped beside me on the log and I put him in my jar. He was all alone in there until I found a couple of centipedes in a rotten part of the log and added them to my collection of jumpy, creepy, crawlers.

I am all rested now, so I continue on my way. I am almost to the top of the incline, to the point where the trees open up into a wide open field.

I will turn around when I reach the open field. I always do. If I didn't turn around at that point, if I continued to follow the trail, I would become lost. The trail branches off into many other trails and I would undoubtedly lose my way.

It was awful! I kept running around frantically with increasing fear, tears streaming down my face, my clothes covered with dust and dirt, trying to find my way back to the wooded area, to the trail that would lead me home. I found it some time later and was relieved. Never would I again go into the open field. Never!

I am staring out into the open space thinking of nothing and everything all at once. My stream of thoughts is interrupted when a large drone buzzes by my face and lands on a patch of tall flowers beside me.

I want him. I carefully but quickly hoist the jar up from underneath him and capture him as I slap the lid on the jar. I've got him. What an awesome addition to my collection. I turn and make my way back home.

I will probably never see any interesting insects or reptiles again, except for an occasional fly, and flies are definitely not interesting. I will remember times I walked in the large forest area at the end of my road when I am in an apartment building on the north side of Chicago. I'll have a clear unchanging scene in my mind of every inch of trail that my feet ever traveled, of the green grass, and of the beautiful trees, flowers, and weeds that provided me with the isolation which I love so much.

I am walking back through the grass that I walked through this morning. I can tell that it is at least noon because the sun is directly above my head as I look up. A single tear is rolling down my face, for my feet are now on the pavement of my road and I have lost a part of me that I will never regain again.

Analysis:

Page 1.   Paragraph 2: Shift from present to past - I am remembering how, as a child, I would run down the hill because I would be so close to my most favorite place in the world. I am remembering running to the spot where the steep wooded incline began.

Page 2.   Paragraph 4: Shift from past to present - I am finished with the thought of catching insects as a child because I am reminded, by that thought, of the insects I carried in my present life.

Page 2.   Paragraph 1: Shift from present to past - I am remembering back when, as a child, I saw three boxer turtles in one day. This is because I see a boxer turtle in my present life.

Page 2.   Paragraph 3: Shift from past to present - I am sitting on a log remembering a time in the past when I sat on the log on my walks. *I am rested up, so I get up off of the log to continue my walk and my past* thought leaves me.

Page 2.   Paragraph 4: Shift from present to future - I think about the open field and how the trail goes up into it. This shift takes place because I am thinking about what will take place when I get there.

Page 2.   Paragraph 5: Shift from future to past - I am thinking about the open field and a time when I got lost when I ventured into the field.

Page 3.   Paragraph 1: Shift from past to present - I do not like the thought of being lost.

Page 3.   Paragraph 3: Shift from present to future - I think about the drone addition and realize that the walk I am taking in my favorite surroundings, will be one of the last I will ever have as a child. I start thinking about what my life will be like in Chicago.

Page 3.   Paragraph 4: Shift from future to present - It is easier to think about things I like that are happening now, rather than face up to the bad things in my life.

#13 Speaking Patterns

Voices

Objective Narrative Voice:

It was another grey, dirty day in the city. The sun was just beginning to peek over the edge of the apartment building as Leo bounced the blue, rubber ball against the dingy brownstone. Most of his friends had moved to better neighborhoods, leaving Leo alone with his mother in the small, third floor apartment. As he bounced the ball, he thought of the fun he used to have before they moved, and his mind wandered from what he was doing. Suddenly, he realized that the ball had not bounced back from the wall. He turned and saw that it was rolling quickly down the sidewalk towards the heavy rush hour traffic, so he bounded after it, not thinking of the danger.

Leo's mother, who had been silently watching her son from the kitchen window, did see the danger, and yelled to her son, "Leo, don't go out in the street, you can get the ball later!"

But, because of the heavy traffic, Leo could not hear her, and as he ran out into the road, oblivious of the traffic, a small car sped directly towards him, the driver slamming on his brakes as he saw Leo in front of him. Leo heard the screech of brakes and looked up, and seeing the car he jumped to the side, but the car slid into him, knocking him to the ground.

Leo's mother, who saw what had happened, screamed and tore downstairs. She reached the first landing and spun around on the rail, losing her footing and tumbling down the short flight to the next landing, breaking her arm severely in the fall.

Out in the street, the driver had called an ambulance from a neighbor's house and was checking Leo to see how badly hurt he was. Leo was conscious, and only badly bruised and scared.

A police car, its siren screaming, pulled up to the accident site and an officer jumped out, ordering people to move out of the way. He kneeled down next to Leo and asked him where he lived and his name, and finding he lived in the apartment building behind them, ran up the front steps to tell Leo's mother what had happened. As he reached the second flight of stairs, he found Leo's mother lying on the floor, holding her arm and groaning.

"Is Leo all right? What's happened?"

"He's okay," said the policeman as he lifted her and carried her to the street, placing her in the ambulance next to Leo. As the doors shut, he thought of how strange the accidents were, and how they were probably connected. When the cop got back to the station, he called Social Services.

When he got home, he told his wife about his day, and she, too, wondered about both accidents. The next day the cop's wife told her friend and that night she read about it in the local newspaper.

Neighbor's Story

I'll say I know what happened. I was right here the whole time. I've known something like this was going to happen. I said to John, he's my husband, works over to the steel mill, I said, "Somethin's going to happen, you mark my words." That Mrs. Harrison don't take such good care of her son. Lot's a times I seen her watchin' the television and her son outside somewhere. And she always talks as if she's doing such a good job of raisin' him.

This morning I was cleaning up the kitchen. It looks out over the yard and the street where Leo got hurt. I was watching him play ball up against the building. I love kids. We never had none, but I always wanted to have some. I think it's John's fault, but you couldn't get him to admit it.

I saw the ball roll down the hill toward the road and heard her yelling about not going in the street. The next thing I hear her door slam and she's pounding down the stairs. That's when I heard the thumping. It must of been when she fell. I hear she broke her arm. Serves her right, I say.

I called the police as soon as I saw all the cars stopped. There wasn't anything I could do to help. And that's all I know about the whole thing, except that boy isn't cared for like he should be. I can tell you that much.

Mother's Story

I had just gotten done washing the breakfast dishes, working on my second cup of coffee, when I glanced out the window and saw Leo running towards the road, chasing that stupid rubber ball.

It was clear that he would most likely get hurt. I pushed open the sticky kitchen window and yelled to him, "Leo, don't go out in the street, you can get the ball later!" But, I guess he didn't hear me, or as usual wasn't listening, because he kept on going, right in front of a car. And when that car hit him, I nearly had a heart attack! I ran out of the kitchen and threw open the door, ripping my dress on the latch, then bounded down the stairs, two at a time.

When I hit the first landing, I grabbed the rail to swing around to the next set of steps, and I guess I just lost my footing, because I fell. I don't really remember things too clearly after that, but I do remember my arm hurting, and worrying about Leo! The next thing I knew, I was in the hospital with a cast on my arm, and Leo was beside me telling me he was all right.

Newspaper Report

Leo Harrison, eight year old son of Mrs. Gertrude Harrison, was struck by a car Saturday while playing outside his home at 513 South Rockdale Road.

Police say that the boy was apparently playing with a ball when it rolled into the street and the youth chased it, running directly in front of oncoming traffic. He was treated and released from Mercy Hospital.

There is also information that Mrs. Harrison, after seeing the accident occur from a window, was injured while running down the apartment house stairs to attend to her son. Her condition is unknown at this time. There were no citations issued at the scene of the accident.

Cop's Story

Honey, I'm home. Got any pop in the fridge? Ah, never mind, I'll look. Boy, am I beat. Seemed like every time I went to sit down today I got a call. I

118

think we had two burglaries, an assault, and a bunch of car accidents. Joan, throw me that pillow over there will ya ? Thanks.

Anyway I got a pretty strange call today. Started out as normal, just a kid hit by a car. I was just getting done with lunch when me and Joe heard the call come in. So, we drove over, cleared out the people, and got the kid an ambulance, You know, standard procedure. He was just bruised, so he showed me where he lived and I walked over to the apartment building to tell his mother what had happened. It wasn't too great a place either. I had to walk up two flights of stairs. But, when I got to the second floor, I see this lady lyin' on the landing, groanin' and holding her arm. Come to find out, she was the kid's mother. Seems that she saw him running to the road and ran down to stop him and she fell. If you ask me, I don't think she takes very good care of the kid, any one who would let some thing like that happen can't be a very good mother. I called social services on this one.

Social Worker's Story

After seeing Mrs. Harrison and her son, Leo, I just had to talk to Mr. Parker about them. I couldn't believe he was recommending that Leo be sent to a place "Where he would be better taken care of," like Mr. Parker said. I had to try to convince him that Leo was fine with Mrs. Harrison, that she really did take good care of him. I gathered up my courage, then walked determinedly to his office and knocked on his door. "Come in," I heard from the inside.
Swinging open the door, I walked in. "Mr. Parker, I, am—"

"Why, hello, Jeri, please, sit down," he interrupted, point-ing at a chair in front of his desk. "What brings you here?"

I looked him in the eye and said, " I'd like to talk to you about the Leo Harrison case. I really think you should review it before making a final decision."

"That's rather bold, don't you think? Remember, you're just a trainee here. You're not even a case worker yet," he said, looking at me with surprise. "You've never spoken out about any other cases, why are you so interested in this one?"

#14 Indirect Information

Old Couple - First Scene

The woman rested her hand on the cold metal railing and sighed. The man placed his warm, strong hand over the cold, frail, shaking hand of the woman. She looked at him and moved closer, then her pale, dull eyes moved across the top edge of the canyon, and stared at the evening sky. The man looked at the woman's face and smiled at her. She sensed his glance and returned the smile, but she didn't speak. She was overwhelmed with the vast expanse of nothing and everything. She looked at layer upon layer of rock, and the tiny river so far below that had spent centuries cutting through the ancient stone. Then she said softly, "I'm not so very old."

The man looked away without answering; he saw a dark, gnarled tree with a halo of orange light about it. The leafless branches reached toward the ground, and even as he watched, three small birds lifted from the tree and flew up into the magenta sky.

The man cleared his throat and pulled the woman into his arms. He ran his fingers through her thin, silver hair and embraced her.

Then very slowly the woman began to shake with sobs. She didn't speak, but clung tightly to the man who held her until the sun slid below the far dark hills. She looked up at his face and said, "Promise me you'll come here again next year?"

Newlyweds - Second Scene

"Come on, Mrs. Williams, we don't want to miss this beautiful sunset. It's almost as lovely as you."

"I'll be there in just a second, Matt," Diana called from the front seat of their car as she searched through her bag for the camera her mother had given her.

"There it is," she said to herself "but, how did this get here?" Along with the camera, she had pulled out her lucky piece; a half dollar-size piece of polished glass. When she had been eight years old, she had found it on the beach while looking for sea shells with her father. It always seemed so shiny.

Diana put the piece of glass in her pocket and slowly made her way towards Matt.

"What took you so long, darling?" Matt asked. "Come here, I haven't had a kiss in at least ten minutes." Diana lightly kissed him on the lips. He put his arm around her waist and pulled her close. "You can do better than that, dear." Diana kissed him again. "Is anything wrong, love? You don't seem as happy as I am."

"I'm, fine. I couldn't be happier. It's just been a long day," Diana answered.

"Well, the day's almost over. See, the sun is barely peeking over the hills. Then the night starts. This is going to be the best night of our lives," Matt whispered into her ear.

Diana put her hand in her pocket and felt the glass. She found the worn spots that she had made through the years from rubbing it so much between her thumb and finger. She had done this every time she felt nervous.

It had gone with her on her first date, she had carried it when she went up to receive her high school diploma and it had gotten lots of use during that first month of college. When Matt proposed, she had run back to her dorm room and searched for her glass piece. She finally found it under her Mickey Mouse sweatshirt and had rubbed it until she stopped shaking.

They could barely see the last rays of sunlight over the mesa. "Come on, dear, let's go now," Matt said.

"No, wait. I want to stay until the very end."

As the sun dropped fully out of sight and the dark shadows sprang up from far below, Diana rubbed so hard on the glass that her finger and thumb began to hurt. she took the small worn piece and rubbed it one last time. She then closed her eyes and threw it into the deep, dark canyon. She turned to Matt, grabbed his hand, and her thumb rubbed the back of his thumb. She said, "Now I'm ready to go."

Woman and Child - Third Scene

The pickup slowly rolled to a stop about eight feet from the viewpoint railing. The brilliant gold sun hadn't yet dipped below the edge of the horizon. The young boy jumped out of the truck and ran to the railing's edge as his mother turned off the truck and slowly got out and walked to join him. They stood there silently for a few moments, and then he reached up for her hand and wrapped his small fingers around her own. She swung her hand back and forth, slowly at first and then a bit faster.

"Know what, Mom?" he asked, his glowing face turning up to meet hers.

"What, dear?" she asked kneeling down to his level.

"Think I'll like it there? I've always wanted a tree house, and Grandpa said he'd build me one."

She laughed and pulled him to her. His out-of-the-blue questions were always so sudden. . .so fresh. The strain and tension had taken a lot out of her, yet the one simple question by the innocent victim of this tragedy had broken the pain. She threw her head back in a deep laugh and then looked at him. "You know what, Son? I think you'll make a fine man-of-the-house."

The deepening darkness hid the wide grin that glowed on his face as the two walked hand in hand to the pick-up truck.

Young Woman - Fourth Scene

Standing before the deep brilliant sunset, it finally hit her. The impact of her new freedom. . .the thrill of discovery and the suspense of the unknown. She leaned forward on the cool railing, resting her chin on her arms. The western sky shone with the deep colors of the spectrum that fell down into the dark purple shadows of the cliffs that stretched for miles in front of her. She reached down and grasped a stone, wrapping it tightly in her palm. Then with a quick throw, she cast it far out into the dusk. Its journey through the darkening space concluded with the distant tiny tink of stone on stone. "I know how you feel, little stone," she said aloud. She quickly looked behind her to make sure she was alone and had not been overheard. With a feeling of relief she saw that she was by herself. When she turned back to the dark, empty canyon she said, louder this time. "Right, alone, but you found others like yourself didn't you, little friend." She laughed at herself and turned back to the east. In that direction the sky was now black and she couldn't even see the outlines of the distant mountains she had just come over.

She stared into the darkness and then turned to face the canyon again, and the sky glowed brightly for a moment just before the sun disappeared.

#15 Controlling Structure

The Hitchhiker

Earl Watson awoke slowly, gradually recognizing where he was, feeling the morning sun's warmth wash over him, and yawned as he listened to the comforting rustle of corn stalks swaying in the early breeze, and stretched as he pictured in his mind the miles and miles of corn rows that reached on either side of the empty highway by which he had spent the night in his worn-out sleeping bag that he was rolling up, the very same one he had received on his sixteenth birthday five years before, and swinging his pack and sleeping bag over his shoulder, walked toward the highway where he picked up a cob of corn that had been lying along the road, peeled off the husk and stared at the kernels of corn, counting the number of rotten or black kernels and slowly rotating the cob in his hands, calculating the ratio of good corn kernels to bad kernels, then estimated the number of cobs per plant and plants per acre, and, finally, determined the number of good kernels per acre. When Earl's eye caught a flash of light far down the road, he recognized it to be the reflection of the sun off of the windshield of a car or truck which was approaching, and he thought if it were to be a car, maybe the driver would be a beautiful girl all by herself lonely and wanting someone to talk to or share her cooler of pop with, but then again, the driver might be a real jerk or some weirdo driving an old beat-up car with a busted radio and lumpy seats, however, if it were to be a truck he would make better time because truckers almost always pick up hitchhikers, and they usually drive in excess of the speed limit on open highways— unless this trucker has been driving all night long and he's too tired to pick up a hitchhiker. The vehicle was about a mile away when Earl recognized that it was a truck, an eighteen wheeler, and if it were to stop for him he would be able to hear the hiss of its air brakes about the time it passed the fifth telephone pole, which was approximately one hundred yards away, he figured, running his pocket comb through his greasy hair and removing the wrapper from a stick of Juicy Fruit gum. He chewed vigorously and his mouth absorbed the pleasant sweet taste, making his gums tingle, and he

123

gazed at the oncoming truck, wondering what the driver would be like and what he would talk about. Swinging his pack and sleeping bag off his shoulder, he looked down the road in the opposite directions fighting how long it would be until he was in Chicago and done with all this hitchhiking. Earl impatiently shifted his weight, kicking little pebbles from the edge of the road then throwing them, one by one, as far as he could out into the cornfield. Glancing up and seeing the truck approach the fifth telephone pole, he listened for the hissing noise that would bring the truck to a halt. It screamed by the pole, not slowing a bit, and Earl looked on discouragingly as the truck passed the fourth pole. He realized the truck's speed was increasing as the whine of its finely tuned engine grew more shrill. He jammed his hands into his pockets and looked disgustedly at the windshield. He was unable to see the driver's features because of the blinding reflection of sunlight. It was nearly upon him now and Earl felt his face redden with anger. The earth beneath him shivered under the truck's incredible weight and speed. He saluted the driver with his hand. "You selfish slob! You stink," he yelled. "Stupe!"

Loud glaring blast... choking stench vibration... shiny black... ear-splitting roar... dirty silver clank.

"Boy, Who needs you?" Earl coughed in the heavy air as the wheels rolled on by. The rig had gone by him as if he weren't even there. It belched dark smoke in rolling clouds that hung in the air, gradually falling to the ground. Earl brushed off his clothes, picked up his pack and bag and took one last glance at the receding truck that was about to go over the top of a hill and disappear. He could still hear the faint rumble, but it was leaving as quickly as the truck that it was coming from was fading from his sight. At last it was gone and Earl took a deep breath and sighed tiredly, for even though he had just gotten up a short time before, he suddenly felt very tired and worn out and helpless, and he wished he would have jumped into the road or something to make the driver stop. How could somebody just drive by and leave him in the middle of nowhere when they could just as easily have stopped, opened the door, and given him a crummy ride to Chicago, which was all he wanted—was that too much to ask? There probably wouldn't be another car or truck for hours or maybe not all day, he thought, turning and checking the direction the truck had come from, wishing he would see another shiny speck, growing in size as it got closer, with a beautiful girl who would pick him up and talk to him about where she grew up, her mother and father, anything at all, it didn't matter to him. And then, maybe they could stop and have lunch somewhere, and he could tell her all about himself his dreams and his plans for the future that he felt would never come true but always sounded so attractive when he talked about them—his house on the beach, his loving wife, a good paying job, a couple of kids, lots of parties, all the good things in life that he wanted, that almost every man wanted but few acquired. A jet flew directly over him, and he looked up at the white trail, then saw the jet itself, which was now miles away from where it had been a few seconds before, the sound of its engines trailing it by at least five seconds, and he wondered what Iowa looked like from up there: green corn fields everywhere, cut by a road now and then, or like a patchwork quilt of shades of green and yellow, or maybe it wouldn't look like either one, he thought, as he started walking, his head down, staring at the center line, planting his feet on it as if he were a tightrope walker and figuring the length of each white dash, and how many dashes in a mile and then how many dashes he would walk over before he reached Chicago.

#16 Creating Characters

Setting

The city of Eltan, Michigan was nestled comfortably on the fringes of Michigan 's fruit belt in Berrien County. It was not actually classified as a city, but all of the townspeople proudly called it the "Fair City of Eltan," or at least they used to. Its population and very existence it owed to its history and the three remaining industrial corporations, one of which had lately been threatening to move south to Texas or South Carolina or wherever. Eltan was a friendly, safe place to live. The crime rate was practically nonexistent, and the scream of sirens usually only signaled an approaching parade. But, it hadn't always been peaceful. One time, six supposed members of Al Capone's gang, passing through by train from Detroit to Chicago, had holed up in the then prosperous Eltan Grand Hotel for eighteen days, and by the time the police were able to restore law and order, twelve people, including five of the six gangsters, had been killed. That was by far the most exciting event in the town's history, and Old Man Smatter who sat out on his front porch down by the railroad station on hot summer afternoons, still told of how he had single-handedly killed two of the gangsters. Old Man Smatter was insane but harmless enough, and local kids would sometimes stop and joke with him when there was nothing else to do.

Eltan's main street ran through the downtown area, all three and one-half blocks of it, passing several small businesses which somehow managed to stay in business despite it all. Most of the buildings weren't occupied by the same business for more than two or three years at a time, so residents weren't surprised when a new store popped up in another's place. In fact, some of the farmers who didn't get into town very often, joked about how Eltan changed every trip. The Diamond's Drug Store and Kroger's Supermarket had been there for almost twenty years, but the old A. & P. was now a bowling alley, its only profitable days being Saturday and Sunday afternoons when it held the league tournaments. There wasn't much else to do in Eltan. The one movie theater, which still had the appearance and presence of a vaudeville show place, had recently closed down because it was falling into decay and the owner simply couldn't afford to make repairs. Most people drove into Kalamazoo for action, it was only forty-five minutes, and there were always plenty of things to do there.

The main street passed over Trail Creek on the edge of town and ran gradually into the "Westside". This was the high ground; the most beautiful homes in Eltan had been built here and they dotted the sides of the gently sloping hills. The main street turned into Clancy Lane on the other side of the creek and began meandering up into the hills. About three quarters of a mile up was a sharp looking, yellow, two-story home with one big elm tree in the center of the front yard. Its branches hung over the driveway slightly, although they had to be pruned regularly so as not to interfere with the basketball goal at the edge of the concrete. A twenty-five foot fishing boat was parked in front of the goal, and a man in his early forties, holding a garden hose in his left hand, was busy on board, scrubbing down the walls and decking with a wire brush.

Bill was stretched out on his bed, a pair of headphones strapped to his ears, his bare feet wriggling to the fast rock beat. He did not hear the screams and laughter coming from the built-in swimming pool directly below his upstairs window. The wall across from him was covered with a huge, nearly life-size poster of pro and college basketball stars in intimidating poses. On the east wall were several pictures of deer, moose, and game animals which had been cut out of *Field and Stream*. The wall behind his bed was occupied by four, five-foot-long shelves, which were crowded with trophies, awards and ribbons which he had won.

Beside his bed was a small desk on which were scattered thirty cassette tapes, several sheets of notebook paper, and a manual typewriter. The floor of his room was carpeted in a deep blue color and cluttered with *Sports Illustrated* magazines, wadded up pieces of paper, a telephone with its cord wrapped around the leg of the bed, three folders containing homework and several letters from colleges which were interested in him for his basketball abilities.

Character Sketch

Bill McClain's tall, slender body was stretched out lazily on the bed, his face hidden behind the latest issue of *Sports Illustrated*. The bed shook slightly to the rhythm of his feet, which were rocking back and forth to the heavy metal beat of the rock music that was pouring into his ears by way of a pair of headphones. His blue eyes scanned the pages quickly; the basketball season was over and he was not interested in baseball, but there were a few good tennis articles. A fly buzzed by his ear, but he didn't notice it until it finally landed on his bare stomach. Bill's rolled his magazine and took aim.

"Dead meat," he whispered mercilessly as he squinted and moved his hand into range, closer and closer until he was within five inches of the target which was unknowingly cleansing itself. Bill waited a moment, poised, ready to strike with lightning quickness at just the right. . .the fly buzzed away.

"Au man. you stupid jerk!" he said in a slightly annoyed tone as he unrolled the magazine and again opened it to his article.   The door opened and Mrs. McClain entered carrying a clean stack of folded socks and underwear. She paused and looked at the floor, which was littered with dirty laundry, sheets of paper, several letters and a couple of high school textbooks.

"Bill, I thought I told you to straighten up this room," she said as she made her way over to the dresser, walking across the floor as if it were a mine field.

"Huh?"

"I said, I. . .Take those things off, I'm talking to you."   "Oh." He removed the earphones and turned off the tape. "What?"

"I told you to clean up this pig sty two days ago."

"I know. I did. But, it got dirty again."

Mrs. McClain flashed a disgusted look at him. "Well, clean it up right now." She started out and then noticed a letter on the floor. "When did this come?"

"What?"

"This letter from Dayton College," she said, picking it up. "I think you'd better find out what they want. Maybe it's something about your basketball scholarship. Have you written them to set up an interview?"

"No, not yet. "

"Why not?"

"I didn't have time," he said raising his voice slightly. "I've been busy. I'll do it later." He snatched his basketball from the desk top next to the bed and expertly spun it on his finger.

"It's almost the end of your senior year and you still don't have a college lined up. Don't you think you'd better take care of some of these things?"

"Take it easy, would ya, Mom? I said I'd take care of it." The ball slipped off his finger. "Gimme the letter, please." She handed it to him and left the room, closing the door behind her with a loud click. Bill rolled over on his stomach and reached underneath the bed. His fingers touched a wire and he gave it a tug. A pile of dirty clothes next to his Purdue University wastebasket jumped. "Ah ha!" Swinging his feet onto the floor, he walked over to the buried telephone. The door opened again.

"Bill, don't you dare make any plans until this room is cleaned up!" She slammed the door this time.

"Geez. What a pain," he whispered under his breath, as he glanced out the window overlooking the swimming pool. The cover had just come off four days ago, and the water looked inviting. Reaching down, Bill picked up telephone and dialed a number from memory. Marty answered on the first ring.

"Hey, Boz."

"Hi ya, Bill. What's up?"

"You wanna shoot some hoop today?"

"Sure thing, Dude. What time?"

"Anytime.,"

"Okay. Hey, did you hear anything from State?"

"No, they must have given up on me, I guess. See ya in a while, Marty."

"Okay."

Bill caught sight of the letter on his bed, and he picked it up, inspecting the envelope. "Nah, it can wait," he said, as he grabbed his basketball and headed for the door.

#17 Short Story

Crows

He walks slowly along the edge of the cornfield, back toward the woodlot. The crows have already seen him (their scout, watching from a tree, called his presence) but continue eating the waste corn left this year. The man knows they feel safety in their distance, knows too, they will come when he is settled.

Dark, rainless clouds bring a wind that moves half-barren trees; the light is weak. The turned field—the rough shape of its furrowed soil and broken stalks—is hard on his bad knee. He wears a brace, but even so it gives, throbs with pain that catches his breath.

He'd seen the flock this morning, driving in from selecting the cattle for slaughter. Through the window of his truck he watched them land in his field—wild, circling, black, their cawing a distant, turning sound. The rest of the morning he spent fixing the old tractor, scrubbing the rust from its underbelly, patching the holes, turning the uneven shape back to straight, smooth lines. He continues to use the old machine that had been his father's, forty years after the farm had passed to him.

The flock was still there when he went to the mailbox. There'd been a letter from his son, away at school. He read that first. His fingers seemed too big to open it, his rough hands too shaky. He read quickly, then his eyes slowed, lost their half-smile. This was something beyond him. He gripped the letter tightly, then loosened his hands and let it lie on his fingers, unsure how to hold it. The thin skin of his face pulled to a frown, fitting the sharp, familiar lines.

His son at nine, running through the cornfield, his hands cupped, held out before him, delicate, careful though his feet are awkward and wild in their placement. "Father," he calls, "Father, I found a bird."

The man comes out of the barn as the boy approaches. "What you got?"

"A bird." He is walking now, holding his hands against his chest. "A baby bird. I found it back in the woods, just on the ground."

"Let's see." The boy lifts one hand slowly, cupping the bird underneath.

"Put that thing down. That's a crow. you don't want nothing to do with that."

"But, Dad, it's just a baby. It's hurt, too."

"I said put the thing down. They're filthy birds. The worst there are."

The boy, hesitating at first, carefully puts the bird down on the dirt drive, his hands still protectively under it, then looks up at his father with anger and fear and disappointment that catch at the man's chest. The crow flaps out of the boy's small hand, one wing beating at the ground, raising a small cloud of dust, the other unmoving, oddly crooked. The bird settles, dust dulling the black of its feathers. Kneeling by it, the boy watches.

His father, seeing the concern in his son, wants to tell him that the bird will be fine, that they'll care for it. He wants to reach out and touch the boy's shoulder, but his hands stay close at his sides. This is only a crow. "Go and get me the shovel." He tries to say it gently, but the words come sharp, too loud. "And then go on in and wash your hands good."

"What are you gonna do?"

"Just go. Now." The boy stands up, walks toward the barn, looks back at the crow, his father, then goes on into the dark building.

His breathing had turned hard, deep. It trembled. The letter became something unmoving and permanent. His eyes closed tightly, he could still see it, the white paper, the shape of the words, the way the folds broke the page unevenly. He thought then of putting it away, willed his hands to do so, thought, 'I will do this now,' but couldn't and waited, tried not to see the words but could not stop himself from reading it again. This wasn't anything he understood, didn't fit the world he knew: the farm, raising the cattle, working the fields, growing the corn he used as feed, the change of seasons—when to plant, and harvest, and slaughter. Everything came together, had a place. He had taken what his father taught him, made his life by it, become secure in it so he no longer had to think about it, only act, and move with the year. But this, now, didn't fit, stopped him, and he found he didn't know where to go, had no sense of direction; he couldn't even tell which way he faced, if the house lay in front of him, or the cornfield, or the near pasture—even the driveway beneath him was nameless beyond the letter.

He noticed something, a sound, that had been continuous, but for a moment, unplaceable. The crows. Their calling became sharp again, from behind. He turned, lowering the letter, and looked at the birds scattered in his torn field. Watching, he was suddenly conscious of his strained breathing He glanced around to see if anyone had heard, or noticed him standing in the drive staring at the paper. He shoved the letter in his pocket and walked to the house.

He set the mail on the entryway table. "Mary," he called, tentatively, heading toward the kitchen. He got no answer, started to call for her again but remembered she'd left in the morning with Mrs. Hitting. At the kitchen doorway he realized that he'd forgotten to take off his coat and boots—something he'd never missed before, a ritual of entering the house he'd followed for years.

Mary would be home soon. She always returned before noon to make lunch.

The refrigerator was loud. He listened to the steady sound. It drew him in, calmed him, distorted his sense of time—every-thing became motionless.

Through the opposite doorway he could see the table in the living room where the photographs were. He knew them by place, and spoke to the one of his father. "What would you have done?

Nothin—I'd never've done this. I'll die same as you." He rubbed his eyes with his fingers "You never saw me; though, takin' this place over. But you knew, you knew I'd never dare not, even with you dead." His voice fell away, the house quiet—he strained to hear the hum through the silence.

He got the gun and his crow call from the den, the owl decoy from the barn and walked to the field where the flock was still at rest, the path around its edge—doing this thing knowing nothing else to do, following what came easiest to him.

The farm is no longer as large as it had been when his father was alive—he'd had to sell land, couldn't support it all. He has never been able to run it like his father, though he's always tried to follow him exactly. It is as if his father had known some magic he never shared, a knowledge now gone lost in the earth.

He pauses, the gun cradled in his arm. Breathing hard, he looks over the field, then on behind him to the road, the house and barn, the pasture where the cattle are, knows very suddenly when his eyes have wandered past the lines of his property, knows too, a feeling that he still owns land that was once his, like a man who has pain in a leg he has lost.

He focuses then on where he is going; the old tree where he built the blind at the end of the field. He caresses the gun with the hand holding it against him, his skin thin and loose the bone clear underneath. Hearing the crows now, he hates them, but their sound is strong, fills him, pushes him on.

He ties the owl to a low branch on a tree twenty feet from his blind. The wind pulls at it slightly, twisting it on the string. Lowering his thin body to the ground behind the blind of piled branches, he leans one hand on the smooth, barkless trunk of an old tree. It has lost all its limbs, its top long fallen: it runs down to its roots, does not rise from the earth. He settles the gun across his lap. A car, its motor low and distant, passes on the road. Some crows move into the tree by the road, then return to the corn. Over the top of the blind, he looks at the owl decoy—this thing the crows will hate and attack and lose their fear of man before, driven mad by the sound of a baby crow's scream.

His back hard against the tree he feels for a moment solid, unmovable, that even the wind is unable to stir his hair; did not hear the creak as his body first pushed against it, the tree now hollow, weakening. He reaches in his pocket for the crow call and brushes the letter. He pulls that out instead. Unfolds it, reads.

When the crows come to the shrill scream, they come a black mass that loses form after form—hearts pounding they attack the owl, try to stop the sound that calls and turns them wild. The man rises with the gun, knowing the moves and actions so well that, even old and weak and stiff; he flows and finds a kind of magic of his own. The birds, swarming the owl, he could just shoot and hit randomly but chooses one instead the shotgun loud it breaks the crows' sound the bird explodes black turns red it falls another blast a second bird this sound takes even the wind.

Then stops. He lowers the gun to load two more shells. He hears his breathing, becomes conscious of it. He feels suddenly that he will stop breathing, that he must force himself to take in air.

There is movement on the ground, under the tree. He looks. The second crow he shot is only wounded. It works itself in a circle, flapping one wing, the other gone. He hears it scream, its voice in pain distinct

133

among the other birds' noise. Its blood wets the dirt. He feels its black eye watch him. The gun is heavier when he aims at the bird, the kick harder when he shoots, the sound harsher.

When the bird lies still, the flock still circling above it, the old man leans over to pick up his son's letter from the ground. He looks again at the dead crow, the spread of black feathers, thinks of the shovel coming down hard, no scream, but he could feel the bones give through the handle, then, turning around, his son's face at the window, watching.

A LOOK AT "CROWS"

This is the best story written by a high-school-aged student that has been turned in to me in my 30 years of teaching. I am very proud of this young person's efforts. It might help you to see the relevance of the exercises in this book if I demonstrate how the skills involved were used in this story.

#1. and #2. "Establishing Location for Narrative Voice" and "Further Exercises in Establishing Narrative Voice Position"

The narrative voice in this story follows the old man. All that is described could have been seen by a person standing next to him. The first line establishes this.

He walks slowly along the edge of the cornfield, back toward the woodlot

We have the area described, the rain clouds, the crows, the fields, but they all could have been seen from where he is standing.

When we go into the flashbacks, we still see the actions from a position that has to be next to the old man.

His son at nine, running through the cornfield, his hands cupped, held out before him, delicate, careful though his feet are awkward and wild in their placement. "Father," he calls, "Father, I found a bird."

The man comes out of the barn as the boy approaches. "What you got?"

"A bird." He is walking now, holding his hands against his chest. "A baby bird. I found it back in the woods, just on the ground."

"Let's see." The boy lifts one hand slowly, cupping the bird underneath. "Put that thing down. That's a crow. You don't want nothing to do with that."

"But, Dad, it's just a baby. It's hurt, too."

"I said put the thing down. They're filthy birds. The worst there are."

The boy, hesitating at first, carefully puts the bird down on the dirt drive, his hands still protectively under it, then looks up at his father with anger and fear and disappointment that catch at the man's chest. The crow flaps out of the boy's small hand, one wing beating at the ground, raising a small cloud of dust, the other unmoving, oddly crooked. The bird settles, dust dulling the black of its feathers. Kneeling by it, the boy watches.

His father, seeing the concern in his son, wants to tell him that the bird will be fine, that they'd care for it.

We even follow the man into his house.

135

He set the mail on the entryway table. "Mary," he called, tentatively, heading toward the kitchen. He got no answer, started to call for her again but remembered she'd left in the morning with Mrs. Whiting. At the kitchen doorway he realized that he'd forgotten to take off his coat and boots—something he'd never missed before, a ritual of entering the house he'd followed for years.

Mary would be home soon. She always returned before noon to make lunch. The refrigerator was loud. He listened to the steady sound. It drew him in, calmed him, distorted his sense of time—everything became motionless.

Through the opposite doorway he could see the table in the living room where the photographs were.

We follow him through his house and barn as he prepares to kill the crows.

He got the gun and his crow call from the den, the owl decoy from the barn and walked to the field where the flock was still at rest, the path around its edge—doing this thing knowing nothing else to do, following what came easiest to him.

We see the crows as he would have seen them.

When the crows come to the shrill scream, they come a black mass that loses form after form—hearts pounding they attack the owl, try to stop the sound that calls and turns them wild. The man rises with the gun, knowing the moves and actions so well that, even old and weak and stiff he flows and finds a kind of magic of his own. The birds, swarming the owl, he could just shoot and hit randomly but chooses one instead the shotgun loud it breaks the crows' sound the bird explodes black turns red it falls another blast a second bird this sound takes even the wind.

Then stops. He lowers the gun to load two more shells. He hears his breathing, becomes conscious of it. He feels suddenly that he will stop breathing, that he must force himself to take in air. There is movement on the ground, under the tree. He looks. The second crow he shot is only wounded. It works itself in a circle, flapping one wing, the other gone. He hears it scream, its voice in pain distinct among the other birds' noise. Its blood wets the dirt. He feels its black eye watch him. The gun is heavier when he aims at the bird, the kick harder when he shoots, the sound harsher.

When he realizes what he has taught his son and why he has received this letter, we are right there next to him and in some way we even see some of the action as though through his eyes.

When the bird lies still, the flock still circling above it, the old man leans over to pick up his son's letter from the ground. He looks again at the dead

136

crow, the spread of black feathers, thinks of the shovel coming down hard, no scream, but he could feel the bones give through the handle, then, turning around, his son's face at the window, watching, learning.

#7. "Reader Identification With Character"

This young author chose to create reader identification in the hardest of the three ways—by creating a character the reader knows so well that the reader understands why the character does what he does. This is assuming that the intended reader is a fairly young person. This may be why I like the story so much. I identify with the old man because I too have a son, and he also is carving out a life for himself that does not include me in his life's work. In some ways I feel like the old man. But for most readers, the third method of identification works. See what we learn about this man that helps us understand him:

He does what he has to do even though he's in pain.

The turned field—the rough shape of its furrowed soil and broken stalks—is hard on his bad knee. He wears a brace, but even so it gives, throbs with pain that catches his breath.

He is a careful workman and takes pride in his equipment. From sentiment?

The rest of the morning he spent fixing the old tractor, scrubbing the rust from its underbelly, patching the holes, turning the uneven shape back to straight, smooth lines. He continues to use the old machine that had been his father's, forty years after the farm had passed to him.

He is much shaken by the letter he receives from his son. He loves him? We find out later in the story that the son has written that he does not want to come back to live on the farm. This reaction by the old man is easy to understand.

There had been a letter from his son, away at school. He read that first. His fingers seemed too big to open it, his rough hands too shaky. He read quickly, then his eyes slowed, lost their half-smile. This was something beyond him. He gripped the letter tightly, then loosened his hands and let it lie on his fingers, unsure how to hold it. The thin skin of his face pulled to a frown, fitting the sharp, familiar lines.

We see that the old man wants to be kind and gentle but does not know how. He is a practical man beset by his failure to make a success of the farm as his father had, and he feels that he must teach his son to be hard and practical so that he can survive.

> *The man comes out of the barn as the boy approaches. "What you got?"*
> *"A bird." He is walking now, holding his hands against his chest. "A baby bird. I found it back in the woods, just on the ground."*
> *"Let's see." The boy lifts one hand slowly, cupping the bird underneath. "Put that thing down. That's a crow. You don't want nothing to do with that."*
> *"But, Dad, it's just a baby. It's hurt, too."*
> *"I said put the thing down. They're filthy birds. The worst there are."*
> *The boy, hesitating at first, carefully puts the bird down on the dirt drive, his hands still protectively under it, then looks up at his father with anger and fear and disappointment that catch at the man's chest. The crow flaps out of the boy's small hand, one wing beating at the ground, raising a small cloud of dust, the other unmoving, oddly crooked. The bird settles, dust dulling the black of its feathers. Kneeling by it, the boy watches.*
> *His father, seeing the concern in his son, wants to tell him that the bird will be fine, that they'd care for it. He wants to reach out and touch the boy's shoulder, but his hands stay close at his sides. This is only a crow.*

He tries to be kind but has had no experience at it. He does not want his son to see him kill the crow for he knows it will hurt him, and he sends him in to wash his hands.

> *"Go and get me the shovel." He tries to say it gently, but the words come sharp, too loud. "And then go on in and wash your hands good."*
> *"What are you gonna do?"*
> *"Just go. Now."*

This is a man of feelings and the capacity for emotional intensity but without the experience or skills to deal with them.

> *He thought then of putting it away, willed his hands to do so, thought, I will do this now, but couldn't and waited, tried not to see the words but could not stop himself from reading it again. This wasn't anything he understood, didn't fit the world he knew: the farm, raising the cattle, working the fields, growing the corn he used as feed, the change of seasons—when to plant, and harvest, and slaughter. Everything came together, had a place. He had taken what his father taught him, made his life by it, become secure in it so he no longer had to think about it, only act, and move with the year. But this, now, didn't fit, stopped him, and he found he didn't know where to go, had no sense of direction; he couldn't even tell which way he faced, if the house lay in front*

138

of him, or the cornfield, or the near pasture—even the driveway beneath him was nameless beyond the letter.

We learn how shaken he is by the experience of the letter. We suffer with him his sense of loss.

At the kitchen doorway he realized that he'd forgotten to take off his coat and boots—something he'd never missed before, a ritual of entering the house he'd followed for years.

We learn that he places great value on family and the sense of continuity of family efforts. We now understand why he is so upset about the letter.

Through the opposite doorway he could see the table in the living room where the photographs were. He knew them by place, and spoke to the one of his father. "What would you have done? Nothin'—I'd never've done this. I'll die same as you." He rubbed his eyes with his fingers. "You never saw me, though, takin' this place over. But you knew, you knew I'd never dare not even with you dead." His voice fell away, the house quiet—he strained to hear the hum through the silence.

#4. "Point of View"

The narrative voice starts this story in present tense.

He walks slowly along the edge of the cornfield, back toward the woodlot. The crows have already seen him (their scout, watching from a tree, called his presence) but continue eating the waste corn left this year. The man knows. . .

He shifts, with a flashback, to past tense.

He'd seen the flock this morning, driving in from selecting the cattle for slaughter. Through the window of his truck he had watched them land in his field—wild, circling, black, their cawing a distant, turning sound. The rest of the morning he spent fixing the old tractor, scrubbing the rust from its underbelly. . .

He puts us in the old man's mind, and we see events of the past as the man sees them even though we see them in third person and not in first person as the man would have seen them. These things we read in present tense.

His son at nine, running through the cornfield, his hands cupped, held out before him, delicate, careful though his feet are awkward and wild in their placement. "Father," he calls, "Father, I found a bird."

The man comes out of the barn as the boy approaches. "What you got?"

"A bird." He is walking now, holding his hands against his chest. "A baby bird."

The narrative voice is omniscient. We are told what the old man is thinking and feeling.

His fingers seemed too big to open it, his rough hands too shady. He read quickly, then his eyes slowed, lost their half-smile. This was something beyond him. He gripped the letter tightly, then loosened his hands and let it lie on his fingers unsure how to hold it.

His father, seeing the concern in his son, wants to tell him that the bird will be fine, that they'll care for it. He wants to reach out and touch the boy's shoulder, but his hands stay close at his sides.

We are even told how the crows feel and what is going on in their bodies.

When the crows come to the shrill scream, they come a black mass that loses form after form—hearts pounding, they attack the owl, try to stop the sound that calls and turns them wild.

The narrative voice is objective. We are never told that the narrative voice feels anything for the boy, the old man, or the crows. This objectivity works for this young author because we are not told how to think about our identification with the old man.

#3. "Senses"

We are given lots of sensory impressions. The author has done a fine job with this. We see and hear and feel right along with the character because of the descriptions.

Dark, rainless clouds bring a wind that moves half-barren trees; the light is weak. The turned field—the rough shape of its furrowed soil and broken stalks—is hard on his bad knee. He wears a brace, but even so it gives, throbs with pain that catches his breath.

Through the window of his truck he had watched them land in his field—wild, circling, black their cawing a distant, turning sound.

He read that first. His fingers seemed too big to open it, his rough hands too shaky. The crow flaps out of the boy's small hand, one wing beating at the ground, raising a small cloud of dust, the other unmoving, oddly crooked. The bird settles, dust dulling the black of its feathers. Kneeling by it, the boy watches.

The letter became something unmoving and permanent. His eyes closed tightly, he could still see it, the white paper, the shape of the words, the way the folds broke the page unevenly.

He noticed something, a sound, that had been continuous, but for a moment, unplaceable. The crows. Their calling became sharp again, from behind. He turned, lowering the letter, and looked at the birds scattered in his torn field. Watching, he was suddenly conscious of his strained breathing. He glanced around to see if anyone had heard, or noticed him standing in the drive staring at the paper.

His back hard against the tree he feels for a moment solid, unmovable, that even the wind is unable to stir his hair; did not hear the creak as his body first pushed against it, the tree now hollow, weakening. He reaches in his pocket for the crow call and brushes the letter.

#6. "Dramatic Dialogue"

There is a fine balance between what the reader needs to know about the characters' relationship and a realistic exchange between a father and his nine-year-old son.

The man comes out of the barn as the boy approaches. "What you got?"
"A bird." He is walking now, holding his hands against his chest. "A baby bird. I found it back in the woods, just on the ground."
"Let's see." The boy lifts one hand slowly, cupping the bird underneath.
"Put that thing down. That's a crow. you don't want nothing to do with that."
"But, Dad, it's just a baby. It's hurt, too."
"I said put the thing down. They're filthy birds. The worst there are."

"This is only a crow. Go and get me the shovel." He tries to say it gently, but the words come sharp, too loud. "And then go on in and wash your hands good."

141

"What are you gonna do?"

Just go. Now." The boy stands up, walks toward the barn, looks back at the crow, his father, then goes on into the dark building.

#7. "Reader Reactions"

Because of our emotional involvement with the characters, we are moved by the events and scenes of this story. We feel for the old man as he watches the crows settle in his field, but are shocked at the image of the shovel squashing the wounded baby crow.

He looks again at the dead crow, the spread of black feathers, thinks of the shovel coming down hard, no scream, but he could feel the bones give through the handle. . .

We are moved by the scene of the shooting of the wounded crow.

He looks. The second crow he shot is only wounded. It works itself in a circle, flapping one wing, the other gone. He hears it scream, its voice in pain distinct among the other birds' noise. Its blood wets the dirt. He feels its black eye watch him. The gun is heavier when he aims at the bird, the kick harder when he shoots, the sound harsher.

#8. "Symbols in Literature"

Symbols are tough. Did the young writer put them there? Was it intentional or an unconscious action? No matter. I see them as reader.

The big one, the crows of course, are a symbol of what is happening to the man and his values as he loses his son and is losing his farm. This is a common symbol in literature. Black, for death and circling birds for impending doom.

The crows have already seen him (their scout, watching from a tree, called his presence) but continue eating the waste corn left this year. The man knows they feel safety in their distance, knows too, they will come when he is settled.

Through the window of his truck he had watched them land in his field—wild, circling, black, their cawing a distant, turning sound.

We see the hope of the boy when he shows the wounded baby crow to his father. The child at this point can be saved by the farmer, as can the crow. But, they both are lost to him.

"Father," he calls, "Father, I found a bird."

The man comes out of the barn as the boy approaches. "What you got?"

"A bird." He is walking now, holding his hands against his chest. "A baby bird. I found it back in the woods, just on the ground."

"Let's see." The boy lifts one hand slowly, cupping the bird underneath.

"Put that thing down. That's a crow. you don't want nothing to do with that."

"But, Dad, it's just a baby. It's hurt, too."

"I said put the thing down. They're filthy birds. The worst there are."

(He) thinks of the shovel coming down hard, no scream, but he could feel the bones give through the handle, then, turning around, his son's face at the window, watching.

The old man is wounded by time and work the same way his farm and equipment are. They are all worn out by life and its challenges.

The turned field—the rough shape of the soil and broken stalks—is hard on his bad knee. He wears a brace, but even so it gives, throbs with pain that catches his breath.

The rest of the morning he spent fixing the old tractor, scrubbing the rust from its underbelly, patching the holes, turning the uneven shape back to straight, smooth lines. He continues to use the old machine that had been his fathers, forty years after the farm had passed to him.

The farm is no longer as large as it had been when his father was alive—he'd had to sell land, couldn't support it all. He has never been able to run it like his father, though he's always tried to follow him exactly. It is as if his father had known some magic he never shared, a knowledge now gone, lost in the earth.

The empty house, pictures of his family and forgetting to remove his boots when he enters the kitchen work as symbols for what is happening to the old man. Notice the white paper of the letter and the contrast with the muted colors of the rest of the farm: the dark barn and fields, the rusted tractor, the silent house, the crying of the birds, and the recurring images of blackness. These symbols all help to create the mood of the story.

#10. "Creating Mood"

The mood of despair and failure is carefully created. We have an old, crippled farmer alone on a failing farm. His hope, his son's return to the home place to help him, is lost with the letter. We see him standing in the driveway of his

143

home and looking out over the bare fields and seeing circling crows. The clouds are dark and roll over the land.

The old man's world is crushing him. It is getting smaller.

The farm is no longer as large as it had been when his father was alive-- he'd had to sell land, couldn't support it all. He has never been able to run it like his father, though he's always tried to follow him exactly. It is as if his father had known some magic he never shared, a knowledge now gone lost in the earth.

#13 "Speaking Patterns"

There is not much dialogue in this story, but the little there is, is very well done.

There are conversations between the man and his son in which this writer demonstrates an understanding of the differences in tempo and tone between these two ages.

His son at nine, running through the cornfield.

. . . his hands cupped, held out before him, delicate, careful though his feet are awkward and wild in their placement. "Father," he calls, "Father, I found a bird." The man comes out of the barn as the boy approaches. "What you got?" "A bird." He is walking now, holding his hands against his chest. "A baby bird. I found it back in the woods, just on the ground." "Let's see." The boy lifts one hand slowly, cupping the bird underneath. "Put that thing down. That's a crow. you don't want nothing to do with that." "But, Dad, it's just a baby. It's hurt, too." "I said put the thing down. They're filthy birds. The worst there are."

He wants to reach out and touch the boy's shoulder, but his hands stay close at his sides. This is only a crow. "Go and get me the shovel." He tries to say it gently, but the words come sharp, too loud. "And then go on in and wash your hands good." "What are you gonna do?" "Just go. Now."

Notice in these two passages the differences in rhythm in the two speakers. There is an upbeat feeling to the boy's sentences: *"Father," he calls, "Father, I found a bird."* The boy's speech is also full of questions. The man's speech pattern, on the other hand, is made of short declarative, imperative and exclamatory sentences.

"I said put the thing down. They're filthy birds. The worst there are." And, *"Go and get me the shovel."* He tries to say it gently, but the words come sharp, too loud. *"And then go on in and wash your hands good."*

"What are you gonna do?"

#14 "Information Given Indirectly Through Description"

We are never told directly what is in the letter that so upsets the old man. We are told that he feels that he no longer can hold onto the farm and make it work like his father did. We see him look over the fields that he no longer owns:

The farm is no longer as large as it had been when his father was alive—he'd had to sell land, couldn't support it all. He has never been able to run it like his father, though he's always tried to follow him exactly.

Breathing hard, he looks over the field, then on behind him to the road, the house and barn, the pasture where the cattle are, knows very suddenly when his eyes have wandered past the lines of his property, knows too, a feeling that he still owns land that was once his. . .

But we are given, indirectly, the information that the son will not be back to help hold the home place together. That is why the circling crows work so well as a symbol of the powers that he cannot control, that are taking away both his land and his son.

#15. "Controlling Structure"

There are many instances in this story where this student has employed what he has learned about the structuring of his words to help the reader see and feel the action as the characters do.

In the passage below we can feel the rhythm of the circling crows. Look at the second sentence: it is broken up with small images, but still holds together—much as a flock of birds does.

He'd seen the flock this morning, driving in from selecting the cattle for slaughter. Through the window of his truck he watched them land in his field—wild, circling, black their cawing a distant, turning sound.

We can feel the boy's excitement when he comes to his father with the wounded baby crow. We can almost see the small boy running by the rhythm of the sentence. The sentence is direct but awkward as is the boy's progress.

His son at nine, running through the cornfield, his hands cupped, held out before him, delicate, careful though his feet are awkward and wild in their placement. "Father," he calls, "Father, I found a bird."

We can feel, by the change in rhythm, when the boy stops hurrying and shows his father the bird.

The man comes out of the barn as the boy approaches. "What you got?"
"A bird." He is walking now, holding his hands against his chest. "A baby bird. I found it back in the woods, just on the ground."

In the two passages, purposefully similar, about the actions of the wounded crows, we can see the actions of the birds, one in the man's memory and the other before the man, and are helped to do it by the structure of the sentences.

The crow flaps out of the boy's small hand, one wing beating at the ground, raising a small cloud of dust, the other unmoving, oddly crooked. The bird settles, dust dulling the black of its feathers. Kneeling by it, the boy watches.

There is movement on the ground, under the tree. He looks. The second crow he shot is only wounded. It works itself in a circle, flapping one wing, the other gone. He hears it scream, its voice in pain distinct among the other birds' noise; Its blood wets the dirt. He feels its black eye watch him. The gun is heavier when he aims at the bird, the kick harder when he shoots, the sound harsher.

Notice the short, staccato-gunshot-like-bursts of information in that last sentence. When the man is shooting the crows, we are given much the same feeling he experiences. The actions are not broken into traditional sentences but are strung together, much as the man must experience them.

The man rises with the gun, knowing the moves and actions so well that, even old and weak and stiff he flows and finds a kind of magic of his own. The birds, swarming the owl, he could just shoot and hit randomly but chooses one instead the shotgun loud it breaks the crows' sound the bird explodes black turns red it falls another blast a second bird this sound takes even the wind.

Notice how, in the next paragraph, the rhythm is broken when he stops shooting. Here we have very short sentences. The action is stopped. We must read the passage that way. To help you understand this, you might read again the last sentence in the paragraph just above and the first two sentences of the paragraph which follows it in the story, the one on the next page.

146

Then stops. He lowers the gun to load two more shells. He hears his breathing, becomes conscious of it. He feels suddenly that he will stop breathing, that he must force himself to take in air. There is movement on the ground, under the tree. He looks. The second crow he shot is only wounded.

Notice that the story's last sentence is long, the rhythm is repeated. With this structure we get the feeling that things go on. This is what the old man is feeling. He sees his actions of the past producing the problems of the present. This young writer understands this well.

He looks again at the dead crow, the spread of black feathers, thinks of the shovel coming down hard, no scream, but he could feel the bones give through the handle, then, turning around, his son's face at the window, watching, learning.

#16. " Creating Characters "

Notice how the physical description of the old man is presented to the reader. It comes as a natural part of telling the story. We see those parts of the man that are significant to his character development.

He walks slowly along the edge of the cornfield. . .is hard on his bad knee. He wears a brace, but even so it gives, throbs with pain that catches his breath. His fingers seemed too big to open it, his rough hands too shaky to hold it. . .The thin skin of his face pulled to a frown, fitting the sharp, familiar lines. . .The man rises with the gun, knowing the moves and actions so well that, even old and weak and stiff he flows and finds a kind of magic. . .

He caresses the gun with the hand holding it against him, his skin thin and loose the bone clear underneath.

Lowering his thin body to the ground behind the blind of piled branches. . . His back hard against the tree he feels for a moment solid, unmovable, that even the wind is unable to stir his hair. . .

This character is shown to the reader by his actions.

When he sees his son has a bird he is interested but when he sees that it is a crow, he says,

"Put that thing down. That's a crow. You don't want nothing to do with that."

147

We are told that he feels for his son but he is not able to act on these feelings.

> *The boy, hesitating at first, carefully puts the bird down on the dirt drive.*
> *. . .then looks up at his father with anger and fear and disappointment that catch*
> *at the man's chest. . .His father, seeing the concern in his son, wants to tell him*
> *that the bird will be fine, that they'd care for it. He wants to reach out and*
> *touch the boy's shoulder, but his hands stay close at his sides. "Go and get me*
> *the shovel." He tries to say it gently, but the words come sharp, too loud.*

We are shown the intensity of his emotional reaction to the letter from his son.

> *His breathing had turned hard, deep. It trembled. The letter became*
> *something unmoving and permanent. His eyes closed tightly, he could still see*
> *it, the white paper. . .He thought then of putting it away, willed his hands to do*
> *so, thought, I will do this now, but couldn't and waited, tried not to see the*
> *words but could not stop himself from reading it again.*

Still, he is conscious of his actions

> *. . . he was suddenly conscious of his strained breathing. He glanced*
> *around to see if anyone had heard, or noticed him standing in the drive staring*
> *at the paper.*

His actions forgetting about his boots when he enters the house lets us know
how upset he is.

> *At the kitchen doorway he realized that he'd forgotten to take off his coat*
> *and boots—something he'd never missed before, a ritual of entering the house*
> *he'd followed for years.*

We are shown how much his life is tied to his past and the land when he talks
to the picture of his father.

> *"What would you have done? Nothin'—I'd never've done this. I'll die*
> *same as you."*

If you look back at the exercise which produced this story, you will see how
most of the rest of the elements of character creation were employed by this
young writer.

For all of these reasons I am particularly fond of this piece of fiction. This
author has utilized well the lessons and activities which produced this book in
his writing of this story.

STORY ELEMENTS
and
HOW THEY ARE CREATED

SETTING: The time and the place the story occurs.

Writers use subtle clues to the time and location of the action. In stories for young readers, a narrative voice might say that it was spring or that it was early in the morning. Writers for older readers assume that their readers will be able to understand locations and times from descriptions and character conversations.

CHARACTERS: The people in the story.

Characters are given full dimension (as opposed to being what are called flat or one-dimensional) by being given personalities which are distinctive (as opposed to being what are called "off the shelf" or stereotypical). This personality is motivated by realistic desires and allows the author to have the characters interact in interesting ways with other characters and situations.

CONFLICT: The forces in the story acting against each other.

These could be characters or elements of nature which would produce a conflict, but both opposing forces could be within one character, which would produce an internal conflict.

INCITING
   FORCE: The action which triggers the conflict.

This does not have to be a major move or an important event. Some small thing might set off the conflict. At this point the sides are drawn and the rules of the conflict are set.

RISING
ACTION: The conflict gains momentum.

Now the forces in conflict are unstoppable in their struggle. The forces (desires of the characters) take over the action and drive the story to its ending.

149

CRISIS: This is the point in the story when the suspense is at its height.

There can be no retreat of the participants. At this time there can be nothing but the clash of the forces as they face each other for the showdown. One must win. There can be no "draw." They are driven to the climax.

CLIMAX: The place in the action at which it is possible to tell the outcome of the conflict.

At this time one side must be seen to be in the position of the loser and one the winner. All of the abilities of both sides have been brought to bear on the conflict and the outcome is determined.

THE CONFLICT: The conflict or "problem" of a story is created/revealed by an understanding of the situation the characters are in, as it is created by the development of one of the following:

- person against person
- person against nature
- person against society
- person against self

In these forms:

1. Person against person is a conflict where two people (for young readers this is usually animals or children) want the same thing, and the conflict (struggle) is over which one will get it. This form of conflict can develop between best friends, a husband and wife, a boss and a worker, two people at opposite sides of some issue or special interest (such as cowboys and sheep herders) and can center on objects such as a bike, a tree house, or oil field or country, or it could be over an intangible thing like an idea.

2. Person against nature is a conflict where one character (it could even be a group) has a struggle with elements of nature. It might be to survive a storm, to fly a plane, climb a mountain, have a picnic on a rainy day, create an ice skating rink when there is no water, find a honey tree, or any of hundreds of other situations in which characters might find themselves.

3. Person against society is a conflict where one character is in a struggle with a group. This could be a person who does not want to do what the group thinks is best or right to do. This character might not want to rob a bank,

150

allow for the building of a toxic waste dump in the county, go to war or pick on an unfortunate neighbor.

4. Person against self is a conflict between two forces within a character. This could be with the body's desire to eat more than it should and the knowledge that this is not a good thing to do, a desire to have something even if it means to steal it and the knowledge that stealing is wrong, a feeling of guilt over something that has been done, a fear of doing something that has to be done, or any situation where a character must or must not do something that is hard.

   1. Protagonist forces or characters are those which want something. This is remembered because the word starts with *pro*. The hero or the main character is usually on this side of the conflict.

   2. Antagonist forces or characters are those which are against or want to stop the protagonist from succeeding. This is remembered because the word starts with *ant* (a variation of anti). This is usually the side of the conflict which has the "evil" person or the bad force, like bad weather or greed or a "big bad wolf."

The strengths of the two sides must be equal or must differ in prescribed ways, for, if there were to be a conflict between a powerful protagonist force and a weak antagonist force, there would be no contest and the conflict would not create suspense. If a professional football team (the protagonist force) were to have a game with a team from a local high school (the antagonist force), this would not be much of a conflict, and the watcher (reader) would not worry about the "good" professional team being beaten.

On the other hand, if a high school football team were to be the protagonist force and were to be pitted against a team of superior ability (the antagonist), there could be much suspense. This is why the heroes in adventure stories are very often alone or do not have strong forces to help them. They must overcome great odds and trick or outwit very powerful "evil" forces or characters to be successful or to get what they want.

The nature of the forces created will determine the type of conflict that takes place.

1. If the conflict is an internal one (one that takes place within a character, such as with a desired act and a guilty conscience), then, for the reader to make sense of the story, this character must be understood. The writer must help the reader focus on this character and what the character's desires are (the

protagonist force) and what there is about the other character (the opposing antagonist force) that is trying to keep those desires from being satisfied.

2. If the conflict is to be an external one (one that is between a character and some outside force, such as nature) then, for the writer to make sense, these two forces—the character and the outside force—must be understood. The reader must be helped to focus on these two forces as the external antagonist force tries to defeat the desires of the protagonist character.

PERSON AGAINST PERSON:

In many stories the conflict is between two main characters. In this type of conflict the two forces are made up of one or more characters who are pitted against each other.

PERSON AGAINST NATURE

Many adventure stories are written with the major conflict between a person and some element of nature. This might be the ocean, the cold of winter, a storm, flood, fire or wind. The story of man's struggle against these large natural forces is fascinating to many people. In order for this type of conflict to be meaningful, the nature of the natural force must be understood. Many writers assume that their readers will understand conditions such as hypothermia or dehydration or how easy it is to become disoriented in a woods, but if the characteristics of the natural force are not understood and not explained, it will be difficult for some readers to appreciate the story.

PERSON AGAINST SOCIETY

A very popular conflict is with a person against a group of people who are in control. Often this group is called society and it may be represented by school teachers and administrators, city government workers, neighborhood council members, the church leadership, members of a club or organization or a government or governmental agency. The writer must help the reader to understand the dynamics of the group and the power groups have.

PERSON AGAINST SELF

Some stories are written so that the main character has what is called an internal conflict. This is with what we call "better judgment" or "conscience" or moral or religious training. The character wants to do something known to be wrong or has done something and now feels guilty about having done it.

FORMATTING YOUR MANUSCRIPT

In the upper left corner of your title page, type your name (not pseudonym), address, phone number and Social Security number. In the upper right corner you should type the word length. These both should be single spaced.

The first page should include the title (centered) one-third of the way down. Two spaces under that type by and your name. To begin the body, drop down two double spaces and indent five spaces for each new paragraph. Have 1 1/4 inch margins around all sides of a full typewritten page. Double space the body of your manuscript. On page 2 and each page to the end of your manuscript, put your last name followed by a comma and the title (or key words) in the upper left corner. The page number should go in the top right corner. Drop down two double spaces to begin the body of the page and follow this format throughout.

If you're interested in submitting to a certain magazine, write to request a sample copy. At this time you should request a writer's guideline. This is important for it will tell you how to format your manuscript and in what kinds of materials that magazine is interested.

If you would like more information on formatting manuscripts, see *Manuscript Submission* by Scott Edelstein (Writer's Digest Books).

QUERY LETTERS

Some editors request query letters. Any contact you have with a publisher should be with a specific person. These people change positions at a high rate, and you should find out before you write anything to a publisher who is the current editor for the type of material you would like to submit. It would be a good idea to call the publisher and ask the name of the person who edits in your area. Queries are usually required for nonfiction material. In such a letter you should convince the editor that your idea is a good one for his readership and that you are qualified to do the job. you should include your previous writing experience plus published samples to prove your ability. This is especially true about any samples that relate to the subject about which you plan on writing.

Your query letter might start with a lead similar to the lead that would be used in the actual manuscript. Next briefly outline the work and include facts, anecdotes, interviews or any other pertinent information that would give the editor a feel for the manuscript. Your goal is to make him eager to read your manuscript. End with a request to write or submit the work. Give approximate length and the date it could be completed. For a fiction query you should explain the story's plot, main characters, conflict and resolution. Just as in nonfiction queries, you should try and make the editor eager to see more of your work.

For more information on queries, see *How to Write Irresistible Query Letters*, by Lisa Collier Cool (Writer's Digest Books)

Some editors would rather review complete manuscripts, especially for fiction. In this case, the cover letter should serve to introduce you and establish your credentials as a writer plus give the editor an overview of the manuscript. If you're sending the manuscript after being told to go ahead and submit your work, the cover letter should serve as a reminder of this commitment.

HOW AND WHERE YOUNG WRITERS
SUBMIT WORK TO PUBLISHERS

Some of the publications listed are not just for children but for adults and have sections for young authors. Some are so small that they will not be in your library. You may have to send to the magazine for a back copy to find out if they publish the kind of writing you would like to submit.

It's important that you send a self-addressed stamped envelope (SASE) with your work when you submit it. If you don't you probably won't get your manuscript back.

If you have fewer than six pages in your manuscript, you might fold them in thirds and send them in a business size envelope. For SASE use a smaller envelope. For larger manuscripts use a 9x12 envelope for mailing the submission and as a SASE. Mail first class.

MAGAZINES WHICH ACCEPT WORK
BY YOUNG WRITERS

THE ACORN, 1530 7th St., Rock Island, IL 61201. (309) 788-3980. This magazine is 99% written by children for ages K-12. Pay is one copy of the issue the work is in. Sample copies are $1.00. Submit manuscripts to Betty Mowery, editor. Manuscripts may be typewritten, legibly handwritten or computer printout. Will report in one week. Uses three fiction pieces (500 words), two nonfiction pieces (500) words), six pieces of poetry (32 lines). Will not accept longer works.

BOODLE, PO 1049, Portland, IN 47371 (219) 726-8141. Offers children invitation to submit. Audience 6-12. Requirements: Include grade when written, current grade, name of school, and a statement from parent that the work is original. 95% of magazine is written by children. Uses 12 short stories (100-500 words), one mostly animal nonfiction piece (100-500 words), 25 poems (50-500 words). Will accept typewritten and legibly handwritten mss.

BOY'S LIFE, 1325 Walnut Hill Ln., Box 152079, Irving, IX 75015-2079. (214) 580-2000. Audience consists of boys 8-18. Requirements are writer must be 18 years old or under to submit. Uses fiction (500 words or less), nonfiction (500 words or less). Pay $25 for mss that are published in Readers' Page column. Will accept typewritten, legibly handwritten, computer printout.

CHALK TALK MAGAZINE, Chalk Talk Publishing, 1550 Mills Rd.,RR2 Sidney, BC V8L 3S1 Canada. (604) 656-1858. Will publish children between 5-14. No pay for publication.

CHICKADEE MAGAZINE, Suite 306, 56 The Esplanade, Toronto, Ontario M5E 1A7 Canada. (416) 868-6001. Is for children aged 3-9. Purpose and interest is in science and nature stories and nonfiction.

CHILDREN'S ALBUM EGW PUBLISHING, Box 6086, Concord, CA 94524. (415) 671-9852. Audience: children ages 8-14.

R-A-D-A-R, Standard Publishing, 8121 Hamilton Ave., Cincinnati, OH 45231. (513) 931-4050. Editor: Margaret Williams. Take home paper for grades 3-6. Christian themes. Do not send fantasy or science fiction. 400-1,000 word mms accepted. Pays on acceptance 3-7 cents word. Write about current topics, issues that elementary-age children understand.

RANGER RICK, National Wildlife Federation, 8925 Leesburg Pike, Vienna, VA 22184. (703) 790-4000. Editor: Gerald Bishop. Audience ages 6-12. Fiction: animal, fantasy, humorous, science fiction. Average word length: 900 words. Pays on acceptance of up to $500 for full-length of best quality. Writer's guidelines free with SASE.

SCHOLASTIC MATH MAGAZINE, Scholastic, Inc., 730 Broadway, New York, NY 10003. (212) 505-3135. Editor: Tracey Randinelli. Math magazine for 7-8-9 grade classrooms. Fiction: Young adults: problem-solving in the form of word problems. Average line length 80-100. Non-fiction: Young adults: cooking, fashion, games/puzzles, problem solving. Nothing controversial. Average line length 80-100. Stories dealing with math concepts and application in the real world are sought. Pays $50-350 for assigned article.

PIONEER, Brotherhood Commission, SBC, 1548 Poplar Ave., Memphis, TN 38104. (901) 272-2461. Editor: Jane Smith. Nonfiction: Young adults: animal, arts/crafts, biography, careers, education, fashion, games/puzzles, hearth, hobbies, how-to, nature/environment, sports. Average word length: 400-600. Pays on acceptance $25-35 for articles. Would like to see teenagers in sports, nature, health, hobbies.

POCKETS, Devotional Magazine for Children, The Upper Room, 1908 Grand, Box 189, Nashville, TN 37202. (615) 340-7333. Editor: Janet McNish. "Stories should help children 6-12 experience a Christian lifestyle that is not always a moral package, but is open to the continuing revelation of God's will." Contemporary, fantasy, history, religious, re-told Bible stories. Do not send violence. Pays on acceptance $250 for assigned articles, 12 cents a word for unsolicited articles. Writer's guidelines free with SASE.

AIM MAGAZINE, America's Intercultural Magazine, Box 20554, Chicago, IL 60620. (312) 874-6184. Articles Editor: Ruth Apilado. Fiction Editor: Mark Boone. Readers are high school and college students, teachers, adults interested in education in writing. 15% of the magazine is devoted to juvenile audience. Fiction: Young adults: history, "stories with a social significance." Wants stories that show that people are more alike than they are different. No religious fiction. Average word length: 1,000-4,000. Pays on publication $5-25 for assigned/unsolicited articles. Interested in material to promote racial harmony and peace.

BOOKS OF INTEREST TO WRITERS
OF CHILDREN'S STORIES

The Children's Picture Book: How to Write It, How to Sell It. Roberts, Ellen E.M. Writer's Digest Books, 1984.
Guide to Writing for Children. Yolen, Jane. The Writer, 1989.
How to Write, Illustrate, and Design Children's Books. Gates, Frieda. Lloyd-Simone Publishing Company, 1986.

How to Write a Children's Book & Get It Published. Seuling, Barbara. Charles Scribner's Sons, 1991.

How to Write and Illustrate Children's Books. Bicknell, Treld Pelkey; Trotman, Felicity, eds. North Light Books, 1988.

Illustrating Children's Books. Hands, Nancy S., Prentice Hall Press, 1986.

The Writer's Essential Desk Reference. Neff, Glenda, ed. Writer's Digest Books, 1991.

A Writer's Guide to a Children's Book Contract. Flower, Mary. Fern Hill Books, 1988.

Writing Books for Children. Yolen, Jane. The Writer, Inc., 1983.

Writing Books for Young People. Giblin, Jarnes Cross. The Writer, Inc., 1990.

Writing for Children & Teenagers. Wyndham, Lee & Madison, Arnold. Writer's Digest Books, 1988

Writing Strands. National Writing Institute. 1989.

Writing with Pictures: How to Write and Illustrate Children 's Books. Shulevitz, Uri. Watson-Guptill Publications, 1985.

MAGAZINES AND PUBLICATIONS
OF INTEREST TO YOUNG WRITERS

Byline. Preston, Marcia, ed. PO Box 130596, Edmond, OK 73013.

Book Links. American Library Association. 50 E. Huron St. Chicago, IL 60611.

Children's Book Insider. Backes, Laura, ed. 254 E. Mombasha Rd. Monroe, NY 10950. *The Five Owls.* 2004 Sheridan Ave. S., Minneapolis, MN 55405.

The Horn Book Magazine. Silvey, Anita, ad. The Horn Book, Inc., 14 Beacon St., Boston, MA 02108.

The Lion and the Unicorn: A Critical Journal of Children 's Literature. The Johns Hopkins University Press-Journals Publishing Division, Suite 275, 701 W. 40th St., Baltimore, MD 21211-2190.

Once Upon a Time. Baird, Audrey, ed. 553 Winston Court, St. Paul, MN 55118.

Society of Children's Book Writers Bulletin. Mooser, Stephen: Oliver, Lin, eds. Society of Children's Book Writers, Box 296, Mar Vista Station, Los Angeles, CA 90066.

BOOKS OF INTEREST TO WRITERS OF ALL AGES

Children's Writer's & Illustrator's Market, edited by Lisa *Carpenter (paper)* $16.95.

Novel & Short Story Writer's Market, edited by Robin Gee (paper) $15.95.

Beginning Writer's Answer Book, edited by Kirk Polking (paper) $13.95.

On Being a Writer, edited by Bill Strickland $19.95.

The 29 Most Common Writing Mistakes & How To Avoid Them, by Judy Delton (paper) $9.95.

The Writer's Digest Guide to Manuscript Formats, by Buchman & Groves $18.95.

Characters & Viewpoint, by Orson Scott Card $13.95.

The Complete Guide to Writing Fiction, by Barnaby Conrad $17.95.

Creating Characters: How to Build Story People, by Dwight V. Swain $16.95.

Handbook of Short Story Writing: Vol I, by Dickson and Smythe (paper)$10.95.

Handbook of Short Story Writing: Vol. II, edited by Jean Fredette (paper) $12.95.

Manuscript Submission, by Scott Edelstein $13.95.

Theme & Strategy, by Ronald B. Tobias $13.95.

Any book store will be able to order any of these books which your library does not have.

Order Form

To place your Writing Strands order, simply fill out this form and send it to us by mail or by fax. If you would like to get your order started even faster, go to the Writing Strands website and place your order online at: www.writingstrands.com.

		Qty	Total
Writing Strands 1 (Book with CD) Oral activities for pre-writers ages 3-8	$15 ea.	____	_____
Writing Strands 2 For students who can write simple sentences, about age 7	$20 ea.	____	_____
Writing Strands 3 Starting programs at ages 8-12	$20 ea.	____	_____
Writing Strands 4 Any age after *Writing Strands 3* or starting program at age 13 or 14	$20 ea.	____	_____
Writing Strands 5 Any age after *Writing Strands 4* or starting program at age 15 or 16	$20 ea.	____	_____
Writing Strands 6 17 or any age after *Writing Strands 5*	$20 ea.	____	_____
Writing Strands 7 18 or any age after *Writing Strands 6*	$20 ea.	____	_____
Writing Exposition Any age after *Writing Strands 7*	$20 ea.	____	_____
Creating Fiction Any age after *Writing Strands 7*	$20 ea.	____	_____
Evaluating Writing Parents' manual for all levels of *Writing Strands*	$20 ea.	____	_____
Reading Strands Parents' manual for teaching literary analysis to all ages	$20 ea.	____	_____
Communication and Interpersonal Relationships Communication skills for students ages 11-18	$20 ea.	____	_____
Full Catalog Starter Set (Save $40) 1 copy of each item above	$195 set	____	_____
Basic Starter Set (Save $55) *Writing Strands 2, Writing Strands 3, Reading Strands,* and *Evaluating Writing*	$75 set	____	_____
Intermediate Starter Set (Save $10) *Writing Strands 3, Writing Strands 4, Evaluating Writing, Communication and Interpersonal Relationships,* and *Reading Strands*	$90 set	____	_____
Advanced Starter Set (Save $30) *Writing Strands 5, Writing Strands 6, Writing Strands 7, Writing Exposition, Creating Fiction, Evaluating Writing, Communication and Interpersonal Relationships,* and *Reading Strands*	$130 set	____	_____

Subtotal _____

Shipping _____
    $6 - Orders $75 of less
    $8 - Orders over $75

Texas Residents: Add 8.25% sales tax _____

Total (USD) _____

Mail your check or money order or fill in your credit card information below:

☐ Visa ☐ Discover ☐ Mastercard

Account Number _____

Expiration date: Month _____ Year _____

Signature **X** _____

Shipping Address

Name _____

Street_____

City _____ State _____ Zip _____

Phone (____) _____

Email _____

Shipping Information

Continental U.S. - We ship via UPS or FedEx ground. Most customers will recieve their orders within 10 business days.

P.O. Boxes, Alaska, Hawaii, U.S. Military Addresses, and U.S. Territories - We ship via U.S. Priority Mail. Orders generally arrive within 2 weeks.

Outside U.S. - Please order online at www.writingstrands.com or over the phone.

Returns

Our books are guaranteed to please you. If they do not, return them within 30 days, and we'll refund the full purchase price. If you decide to return your books, please pack them securely. We cannot issue refunds for books that are damaged.

Privacy

We respect your privacy. We will not sell, rent, or trade your personal information.

Inquiries And Orders

Phone: (800) 688-5375

Fax: (888) 663-7855 TOLL FREE

Write: Writing Strands
                624 W. University Dr., #248
                Denton, TX 76201-1889

E-mail: info@writingstrands.com

Website: www.writingstrands.com

To order even faster, visit
www.writingstrands.com

Prices valid through 12/31/12